AF470512

A Walker on the Cleveland Way

CLEVELAND WAY

A Walker on the Cleveland Way

A Visual Experience by Colin Walker

PENDYKE PUBLICATIONS

Published by Pendyke Publications,
        37 Pendyke Street,
        Southam,
        Warwickshire.
        CV33 OPE

Printed by Blackwells in the City of Oxford.

ISBN 0 904318 09 5

The author gratefully acknowledges the assistance of Mary Comber, Audrey Dixon, Duncan Jeffray and Joanna Monaghan who checked some of the information and also his son Martin who as always provided tolerant and affectionate company on the long walk.

A WALKER ON THE CLEVELAND WAY

As long distance footpaths go the 100 miles of the Cleveland Way from Helmsley to Filey Brigg is a genial and varied walk following for much of its course the cliffs along the edge of the North Yorkshire Moors. The path is often well walked and clearly defined and compared with the linear 'endlessness' of the Pennine Way with its almost relentless commitment of direction, the Cleveland Way being a more circuitous route takes in all points of the compass so that whichever end is chosen to start from the walker can enjoy the sun (if it shines!) both in front and behind.

The Yorkshire Moors are a compact 'block' of hills covering an area some 20 miles from north to south and 35 miles across and except along their north-eastern coastal edge they look out over extensive low-lying vales. To the south the Vale of Pickering; to the west the Vales of York and Mowbray and to the north the Tees-side plain.

The solid rocks of the moors are a unifying feature having all been laid down during the Jurassic period and pretty well the entire sequence is exposed at one place or another during the walk. Geological unity does not mean uniformity, however. The beds that make up the Jurassic group are quite diverse and as the strata generally rises towards the north-west older rocks emerge from below their successors to provide a change of cover. Thus the white Corallian limestones of the hills in the south of the region give way to the darker rocks of the Middle Jurassic in the Cleveland Hills.

Another important element in the shaping of the moors were the abrasive forces of the Ice cap which gouged out the valleys and whose melt waters produced some impressive spillways. A number of examples are met with north east of Osmotherley and their effect on the landscape can be both seen and felt.

Like any long distance walk the Cleveland Way provides great riches for those whose values are measured in the soul rather than the pocket. Its remarkable mixture of experience includes the airy crop and pasture lands of the dry Corallian Hills, the whispered utterances of dense forest plantations, the liberties of the open moorland, and the delights and frustrations of a splendid but popular coastline. Above all its attributes are its cliff-top views whether back over Helmsley to the Vale of Pickering, across the Vales of York and Mowbray to the Distant Pennines; Northwards over the industrial sprawls of Tees-side or out over the coastal sea lanes where ships great and small ply their cargoes and on a clear day remain in view for what seems like an age.

Racing form, afforestation, fossil type and structure, geological formations, industrial archaeology, gliding techniques, crop utilisation, pre-historic burial sites and defences, coastal erosion, marine and inshore life, livestock trends, meteorological phenomena, novelty golf, birds (feathered and in bikinis!) and Bingo are just a few of the opportunities available for study on this walk without the need to stray far from the path.

The major changes of direction made by the Cleveland Way serve to break it up into convenient sections for description. The first covers the walk from Helmsley to Sutton Bank; with the optional 'appendage' to the Kilburn White Horse. The northward leg takes in the Hambletons from Sutton Bank to Osmotherley then eastwards from Osmotherley to Kildale and on from Kildale to the coast at Saltburn. Finally, the long 45 mile coastal stretch down to Filey Brigg is afforded relieving breaks at Whitby and Scarborough.

It might seriously be questioned whether the merits of the walk along Filey Brigg really compensate for the heavily populated and caravanned scenery between Scarborough and Gristhorpe Bay and one does wonder whether a route back to Helmsley from Scarborough might not have been a better alternative. The use of the trackbed of the closed railway from Seamer Junction to Helmsley via Pickering would certainly have been one possibility and indeed a complete Cleveland Way circuit would seem to have much to commend it.

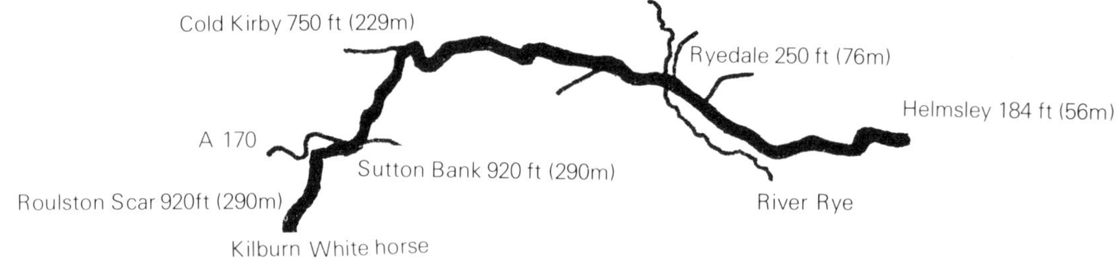

Helmsley to the Kilburn White Horse

HELMSLEY TO THE KILBURN WHITE HORSE

8 ½ miles (13.5 km)

The start of the Cleveland Way is very much taken up with getting to the western edge of the moors at Sutton Bank.

Striking off from the amiable market town of Helmsley in Ryedale, it climbs away along a clear course skirting crops and threading plantations to the top of Whinny Bank only to descend back into Ryedale again. A stretch of metalled road takes it within sight of the idyllic ruins of Rievaulx Abbey.

In its dedication to a westerly progress Ryedale is relinquished in favour of tree-clothed Nettledale and Flassendale from where a short scrambled climb through head-high growth brings one onto the arable heights leading to the breezy village of Cold-Kirby — a significant name in the winter months.

A brief return to lane and field paths then brings the walker past Hambleton House and its stables to the main Thirsk-Scarborough road. At the strategically placed Hambleton Hotel the thirst can be quenched, the energy refuelled and the spirits revived during the licenced hours.

Mercifully, the encounter with the busy A170 is a fleeting one and a plantation track quickly leads one through the pines to the cliff edge of the moors.

The arrival at the edge is a potent moment and time to absorb it should be allowed. In suitable weather conditions the first of what should become a continuum of splendid views presents itself away to the west over the Vale of York to the distant Pennines.

This moment of natural climax is often accompanied by an impressive demonstration by that invisible element — the wind. The Hambletons rise very abruptly from the vale offering a sudden obstruction to breezes that have gathered pace unhindered over the placid levels below. The result is that on meeting the 'wall' they are compressed and thrust upwards with some force.

One doesn't need to observe the virtuoso performances of the gliders overhead to be aware of the phenomenon. It can be felt. The cordial currents which cooled the sweat on the way out from Helmsley can become quite aggressive along this edge.

The optional 'extra' of walking round the promontory of Roulston Scar to the Kilburn White Horse and back adds some two miles to the Cleveland Way. As a popular pilgrimage it follows a well trodden path along the edge of the glider field whose operations are fascinating to watch but decidedly time consuming.

The white horse itself is disappointing because its scale is such that it can only be totally comprehended from a distance. Standing above its nose, its back or its tail tends to be a 'hard-core' rather than an equestrian experience!

What is not disappointing is the view. The white horse presents its profile to the south and this panorama 'round the corner' as it were, enables one to enjoy the nearby and related Howardian Hills and the distant chalk wolds beyond Malton.

1. Helmsley. A pleasant point of departure particularly on a market day.

2. Starters order. The signpost opposite the church.

3. A sample of stiles on the way out of Helmsley whose 13th century castle keep diminishes with distance.

4. Gaining height and some cooling breezes. On the skyline beyond Helmsley is the distant line of the chalk wolds.

5. An introduction to the local style of gate fastening.

6. Concrete hut foundations of the war time refugee camp in Duncombe Park woods.

7. Looking south from Whinny Bank down into Ryedale. Notice the mature deciduous wood topping the conifer planted bank.

8. Selective weed threat from an unselective spray.

9. The 'way' beckons on past Whinny Bank Wood.

10. Select weed varieties growing very handsomely beside the path.
Burdock

11. Nettles.

12. The road down to Ryedale and Rievaulx.

13. Oak timber harvest from Abbot Hagg Wood beside the road.

14. Rievaulx Abbey seen from over the hedge.

15. The River Rye flowing beneath the road.

16. Cottage, washing and cabbage patch near Cross Green.

17. Entry to the forest track below Noddle Hill.

18. The track up Nettle Dale.

19. Limestone stream company.

20. The approach to the Flassendale 'turn'.

21. Flassendale where a signpost directs the Cleveland Way up the valley side.

22. Head-high parsley greeting on the scrambling climb.

23. Effort's end. The bank top and a view back over Flassendale.

24. The view north east from Low Field Lane looks across to the Tabular Hills beyond Ryedale.

25. Low field Lane. The road to Cold Kirby.

26. Tread combinations near the village.

27. Cold Kirby arrival.

28. Cold Kirby departure. A glance back down the village street.

29. Cote Moor Road rising up the contours towards Hambleton House. Another retrospect to the north east looks over Cold Kirby now concealed by its sheltering trees. In the distance are the Tabular Hills.

30. Cote Moor spruce plantation from the path near Hambleton House.

31. Plantation harvest. A stack of fence posts await transport.

32. The A 170 main road near the Hambleton Hotel. The Cleveland Way takes to a short stretch of forest track to the left of the gliding club sign.

33. The Hambleton edge at last! This view looks out to the south west over the conical Hood Hill to the Plain of York. The cliff on the left is Roulston Scar.

34. The vista to the north west. Beyond Whitestone Cliff and Gormire lake the miles spread away.

35. A defeated larch tree on the way round to Roulston Scar.

36. The cliff edge near Roulston Scar looking north west.

Terrestrial and aerial activity on the way round to the White Horse.

37. Bilberry picking

38. Glider winching.

39. The Kilburn White Horse and the view to the south over the Howardian Hills to the distant chalk wolds.

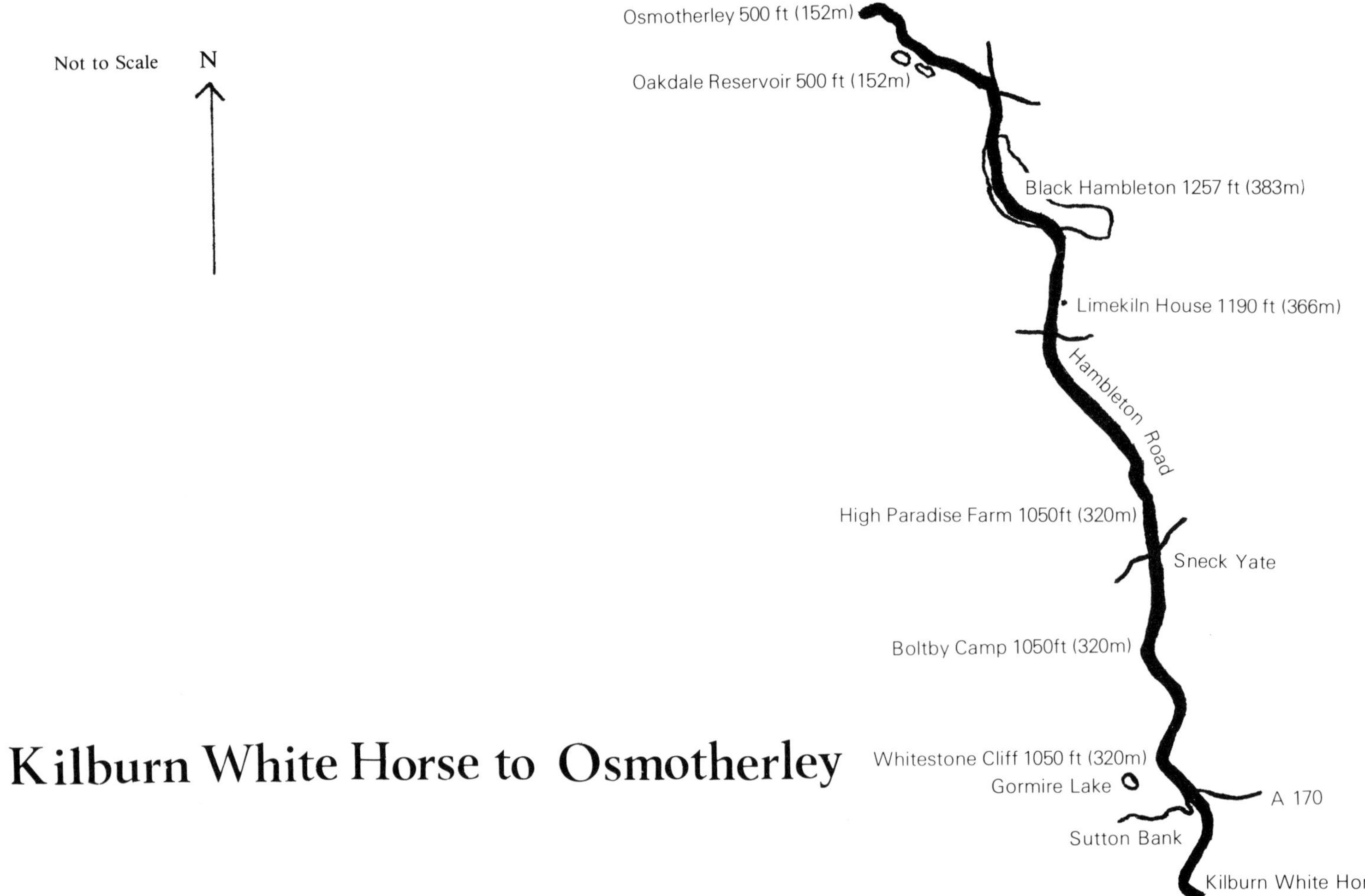

Kilburn White Horse to Osmotherley

THE KILBURN WHITE HORSE TO OSMOTHERLEY
13 miles (20 km)

Retracing the steps back over Roulston Scar and past the glider field the path returns the walker to the main road at the top of Sutton Bank. As a place of popular appeal Sutton Bank's reputation is immense and deservedly so since few main roads offer such a vista and also the 'soft life' amenities with which to enjoy it. It is here, among the cars, coaches, ice creams, Coca Cola and the toilets that the northbound leg of the Cleveland Way really begins.

With suitable haste it does a rapid disappearing act by taking to a leafy path along the cliff tops of Sutton Brow and Whitestone Cliff, a name which amply describes the Corallian Limestone forming them. On porous, turf covered ground the going is usually dry and exhilarating passing high above Gormire Lake in its natural 'bowl' while away to the west is that magnificent sweeping vista.

It is on the open tops away from the distractions of modern living that one can begin to absorb the spirit of these hills and sense their Pre-Historic significance. In many parts of Britain the watersheds, ridges and scarp edges of uplands were utilised for transport and communication routes by our Stone, Bronze and Iron Age ancestors. Bad drainage encouraged and supported a wilderness of growth and swamp down in the clay vales which, in turn provided convenient cover for a variety of uncharitable livestock. Height in those days often meant safety while the commanding views resulting from the clearing of forests after the Bronze Age also afforded a measure of security in the event of guerrilla activities.

The dry limestone tops of the Hambletons must have played a notable role in the network of ancient trackways as well as supporting resident communities. For the walker who can read the landscape the evidence is there to see in burial mounds long and round, in mysterious dykes like the Cleave Dyke which keeps close company with the Cleveland Way for over two miles, and in hill fortifications like Boltby Camp.

Other, more recent, earthworks of the extractive kind are also present like the abandoned quarries above Boltby and Kepwick where stone was quarried for lime burning or for road metal and building.

On Sneck Yate bank the route crosses a road and after a stretch of plantation cover it emerges to join the track leading up to High Paradise Farm (quite an apt name!). Passing the farm on its north side the 'way' continues along the farm road for about a field's distance and approaches a gate beyond which crosses an impressive green road. Impressive because the width between its limestone walls is almost of motorway dimensions.

This is the famed Hambleton Road, an historic drovers road. For centuries it was used to move livestock down the country from Scotland and the north to the cattle fairs and markets of eastern and southern England. From Sutton Bank to Sneck Yate top it is a metalled road but here where the wayfarer turns to join it, it is essentially still a foot road and for the next six miles it provides a broad and bracing walk. The first stage crosses through an 'arm' of Boltby Forest following which the turf road surges on beside a splendid white-stone wall past the rubble remains of the inn, Limekiln House, to Whitestones. Here the route, swinging to take the west shoulder of Black Hambleton Hill, descends from the heights down into Oakdale.

The drovers road on Jenny Brewster's Moor becomes motorised once again and so the Cleveland Way, with a suitably purist gesture, turns westward down the slope into a jungle of heather and bracken where all trace of a footpath is briefly shed. By spring, wall, stile, gate, tree trunk, reservoir road, electric fence and the Cod Beck it eventually clambers up the steps of Middlestye Bank to Osmotherley where a covered entry in a terrace of houses deposits the walker right into the market square.

Osmotherley signals the end of a distinctive stage of the Cleveland Way because the white limestone hills are about to be exchanged for the darker lias limestones of the Cleveland Hills which lie ahead.

40. Sutton Bank top.

41. The invitation to leave it!

42. Discreet exit.

43. Notice of popular conservation above Garbutt Wood.
A contradiction in terms?

44. Whitestone Cliff.

45. A cliff edge hawthorn lives to fight it out with the weather. This is a wonderful study in natural tenacity, courage and stamina.

46. A passing greeting from an eye level crop of willow herb near Whitestone Cliff.

47. Quarry and tumulus earthwork disturbances to the east also mark the course of the Cleave Dike.

48. Gormire Lake

49. A view back from the top of Thirlby Bank takes in the symmetry of Hood Hill.

50. The Cleveland Way turns to negotiate the 'bay' of Hambleton Down. Two Bronze Age round barrows 'pimple' the plateau top to the left of the picture.

51. A more northerly view takes in the promontory of Boltby Scar and the continuing escarpment of the Hambletons beyond.

52. Tumulus close-up. A silent witness of an ancient civilisation.

53. A determined growth demonstration by a wayside Carline thistle.

54. A further example of cliff top endurance displayed by a dwarf larch tree on Boltby S

55. The gate beyond Boltby Scar. Behind the wall is the old quarry while to the left screened by its protecting trees is High Barn.

56. Boltby quarry where stone was extracted for road metal,
until the end of the second world war.

57. The concrete and iron foundations which once supported the aerial
ropeway down which the stone was lowered.

58. A homing bird seeks the cover of the pines in this late evening shot taken from High Barn looking across to neighbouring Kirby Knowle Moor and beyond to the distant Pennines. Overlooking Wensleydale is Penhill Beacon while to the extreme left the peaks of Great and Little Whernside lift themselves into faint supremacy.

59. A look back up the rise to High Barn from near the Sneck Yate road finds a strong direction indicator laid out in stones by person(s) unknown. It is, however, suggesting a return and there's no going back.

60. The road down Sneck Yate bank. On the other side a sign post points the 'way' into the plantation.

61. Milk Market contributions. An expert in cunning camouflage spies upon the unsuspecting wayfarer on the way down to the High Paradise Farm road.

62. Another member of the same herd gives way with great reluctance a little further on.

63. Another late evening photograph looks across to the Pennines through a gap in the thrusting growth.

64. Mrs Bosomworth at High Paradise Farm provides early morning refreshment for some mixed custom.

65. High Paradise Farm — a backward glance.

66. Another retrospect through the gateway where the road from High Paradise gives on to the Drover's road.

67. The Hambleton Drover's road. The way ahead.

68. Boltby Forest. Gate entry.

69. Gate exit leading onto Little Moor.

70. The stump of Steeple Cross beside the road.

71. Round barrow on Little Moor.

72. The Drover's road — an open invitation.

73. A view to the west over the Vale of Mowbray from the gate where the moorland road from Kepwick to Hawnby crosses the Hambleton road.

74. Collapsed walls near Limekiln House. The Cleveland Way crosses the picture from left to right.

75. The heaps of stone marking the site of Limekiln House, a lonely inn once frequented by drovers, quarrymen and lime burners. It closed its doors before the turn of the century.

76. Whitestones which gives entry to Black Hambleton. The path here takes a sharpish turn to the left.

77. The Drover's road skirting the shoulder of Black Hambleton.

78. Death from natural causes but in normal surroundings. How much better than the abattoir.

79. The view south west back to Kepwick Moor.

80. The 'way' commences its descent to Oakdale.

81. The gradient steepens. The line of hills crossing the picture ahead will soon be sampled! To the left of the path is the summit of Beacon Hill on Scarth Wood Moor which can be seen drifting down to the cleft of Scarth Nick which is conspicuous to the right. In the right distance are some visible signs of Tees-side industry.

82. Another vista to the north west over Osmotherley, Swinesty Hill and the Vale of Mowbray.

83. Black Hambleton. Heather sample beside the path.

84. Rough going for sore feet.

85. Abreast of Black Hambleton's mass a view to the north east becomes available and the 'toppings' of Carlton and Cringle moors.

86. A respectful appraisal of Black Hambleton from a now sandy surfaced path.

87. Oakdale Head near the road on Jenny Brewster's Moor. An ideal place for a motorised picnic among the rushes.

88. Oakdale Head where the motor road takes over the Drover's road for a lengthy stretch. The footpath can be seen being directed away to the left.

89. The Cleveland Way ill defined on the way down to the reservoir which is plainly visible as is Osmotherley.

90. The spring line. One of the springs feeding the Oakdale Beck.

91. The wooded approach to the reservoir.

92. Oakdale Reservoir.

93. Oakdale Reservoir — overspill channel.

94. Oakdale Farm — abandoned in the interests of pure water.

95. A glimpse to the west on the way across the fields to the road and White House Farm.

96. The entrance to White House Farm where an electric barrier, white gat and stile make for a degree of confusion

97. Cod Beck descent and crossing.

98. The ensuing stepped climb up through the trees.

99. The top of the steps and some closer evidence of Osmotherley.

100. Osmotherley. Stone stile approach.

Narrow alley entry.

101 Osmotherley.

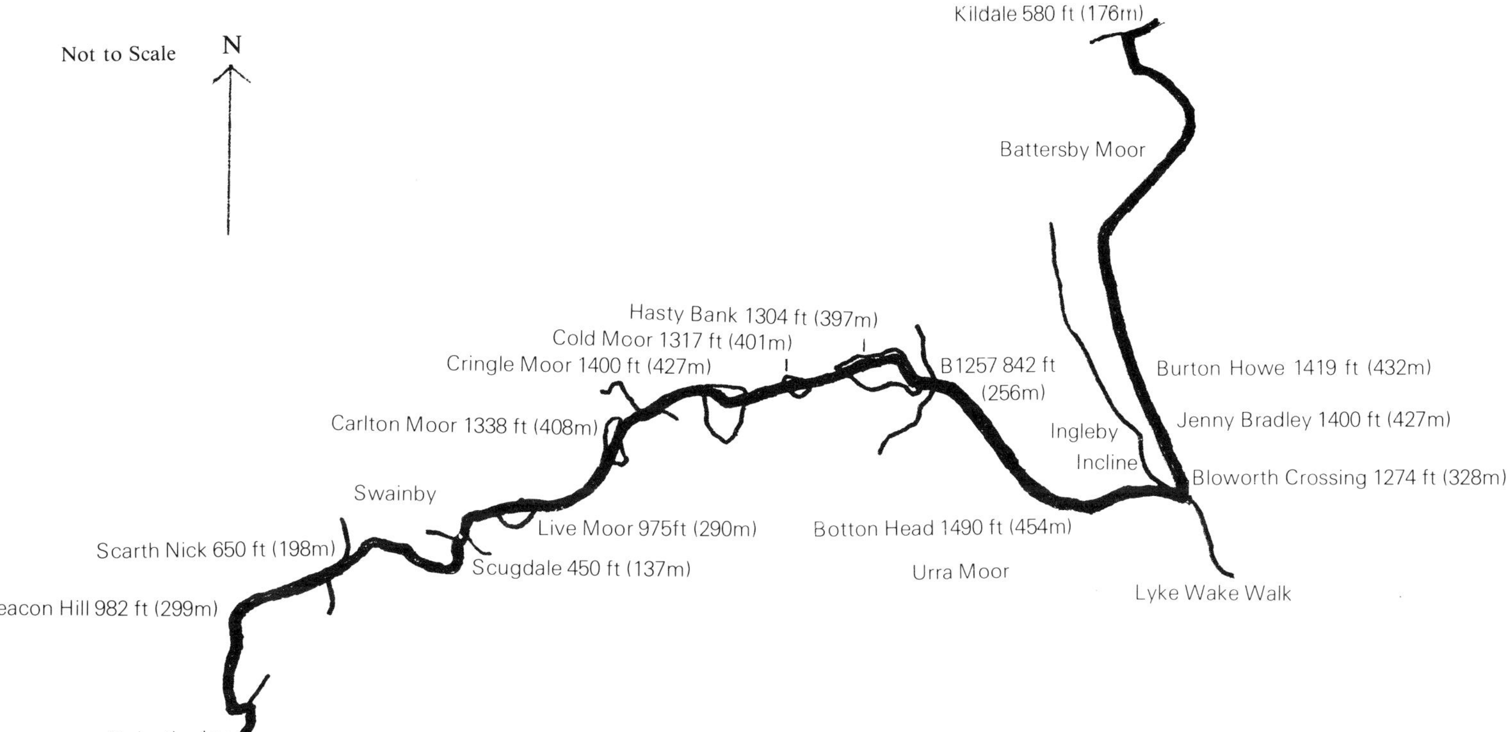

Osmotherley to Kildale

OSMOTHERLEY TO KILDALE

20 miles (32 km)

The exit from Osmotherley is northwards up the Swainby road to the top of the village where the Cleveland Way is directed west round the side of Rueberry Hill. A fine view back to Black Hambleton and the whitestone moors is a compensation for the exertions.

Reaching the edge near Chapel Wood Farm the path resumes a generally northerly progress with magnificent, uninterrupted distances spreading away over the Vale of Mowbray. Then, climbing steadily through another patch of forest it 'happens upon' a cluster of television boosters busy peering over the Tees-side plain from above the trees.

These symbols of advanced telecommunication or rather their surrounding foliant cover introduced a memorable and lasting episode in the author's expedition for it was here in the shade of bracken, gorse and pine that he first encountered the FLIES! By the hundred they awaited with relish any hapless, sweat saturated traveller to arrive on the scene and having selected their victim they then launched an ambush of the most massive proportions. Nor were they 'normal' flies but a particularly persistent North Yorkshire strain which defied all attempts to deter and deflect. So alarming was their personal attention that the author developed a definite 'Fly complex' and was quite convinced that a particularly malicious squadron of these aerobatic pests remained with him all the way to Filey Brigg seeking cover overnight and joining him again each morning after bed and breakfast!

The triangulation point on Beacon Hill soon follows the T.V. station. It marks the start of the Lyke Wake Walk which combines with the Cleveland Way for the next 12 miles. It is also a point of some emphasis because here the route takes a clear course towards the east, following the north facing edge of the moors. As the path declines towards the dip of Scarth Nick (one of the Ice Age spillways) the wayfarer is able to look out over the Leven plain and across to the North Eastern group of moors beyond Kildale whence he is bound.

One result of following a circuitous course if that of the 'persistent image' like the 1000 foot T.V. mast on Bilsdale West Moor which has been visible since the very early stages of the walk and is still prominent to the south. It is now joined by another visual feature over to the north east — a natural one this time, but with some man-made modifications. It is the delightfully named hill Roseberry Topping which stands detached from the main body of the moors and whose quarried and abrupt conical form is immediately evident even though here it is softened by distance.

The return to frondescent growth at the foot of Coalmire brought some massive reinforcements to the winged provocateurs who had conceded no let-up since leaving Arncliffe Woods. Together they provided a constant companionship of torment through the lanes and paths above Swainby where the 'way' takes to a wooded track along Scugdale for nearly a mile finally drifting down to ford a beck and cross the road close to Hollin Hill farm.

The energetic exploitation of Cleveland's natural resources in the 19th century made the quarrying of stone in the Hambletons a mild operation by comparison. In Scugdale both iron and jet were sought and vigorously extracted and a rather less pollution-conscious age has left behind its tips of spoil together with the earthworks of a mineral tramway.

The gradient out of Scugdale onto Live Moor is a sharp one. In something like 230 yards it climbs over 200 feet and on reaching the top the path takes up its cliff edge position again. Live Moor gives way to Holey Moor which in turn leads onto Carlton Moor whose scoured and scraped summit is also used for gliding. At 1338 feet it is the highest point so far on the Cleveland Way.

The undulations are now somewhat conspicuous as the 'way' crosses the spillway dips between the moors. The descent from Carlton Moor is followed by a lung-demanding climb onto Cringle Moor, which rewards with some superlative views and an official seat to enjoy them from. Cold Moor follows Cringle and then comes Hasty Bank where an intriguing rocky community called the Wain Stones, welcomes the climber onto the top.

At the bottom of the down grade from Hasty Bank is the motor road from Helmsley to Stokesley, which has travelled up Bilsdale and perhaps some compensation for the mobile hardware it inflicts is a car park cafe a few hundred yards along the road to the North.

The Cleveland Way crosses the road on Clay Bank and passing through Haggs Gate it climbs first beside a wall and then continues to gain steady height onto the open moor. A mile and a half on and a triangulation point appears near the stone surfaced track with two elder statesmen standing alongside it. These earn a moment's diversion because they announce the summit of Botton Head the highest point on Urra Moor and indeed at 1489 feet the 'peak' of the whole walk.

There is a solitude up here almost of Pennine proportions, that is until the walker reaches the substantial remains of the railway line which once brought iron ore out of Rosedale. On reaching the edge of the moors the loaded wagons used to be lowered by rope down the 1 in 5 incline to the plain below and the earthwork gradient is still very much in evidence. The Cleveland Way uses its trackbed as far as Bloworth Crossing where the rough moorland roads from Kirkbymoorside to Stokesley used to cross the line. The 'way' parts company with the Lyke Wake Walk here by a sharp V turn at the crossing to recover a northerly course along the edge of Ingleby Moor and in doing this it enters the main block of the Cleveland Hills.

Over some five miles the path drifts down into Kildale with inspiring views ahead of Easby Moor and Roseberry Topping and to the west across the re-entrant valley to the line of moors that have been walked. From its first sighting on the way down from Beacon Hill to Coalmire, Roseberry Topping has gradually taken on a more impudent form. Now we are closing the distance its character becomes much more one of arrogance as it rears up from the Cleveland Plain like some enormous solid crested wave. It is not a benign creature!

Walkers should not anticipate Kildale with strong re-victualling fantasies. It is a quiet, serene village of sparse and scattered dwellings and is non-alcoholic though it does boast an unstaffed railway halt on the Middlesbrough — Whitby line.

102. Departure to the north. The view back over Osmotherley from the path on Rueberry Hill with Black Hambleton dominating the skyline.

103. A westerly outlook through the willow herb. Below is Siddle Farm and beyond the A19 which for a few miles provides an audible and visual reminder of 'that other way of life'.

104. The path curving round near Chapel Wood Farm passes a retired railway van now a store for sacks of dressing and fertiliser.

105. The magnificent view to the north west towards Teesdale and the northern Pennines.

106. A glance back at the gate that delivers the 'way' into Arncliffe Wood

107. The path up through the plantation.

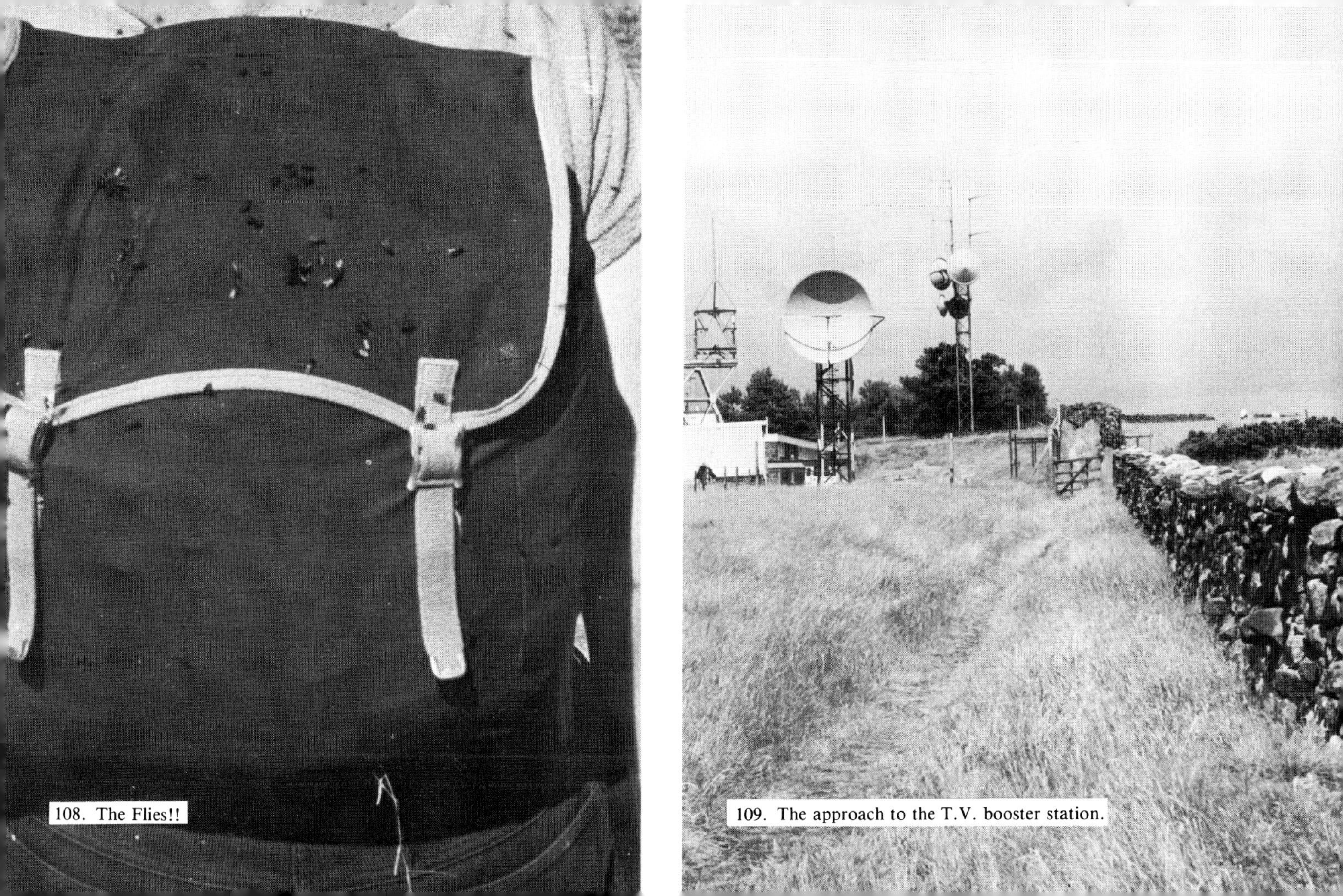

108. The Flies!!

109. The approach to the T.V. booster station.

110. Media for the masses. A close up of the TV 'furniture' erected on the site of Brass Cottage.

111. The view south looks back over Oakdale to Over Stilton Moor.

112. The Ordnance Survey post on Beacon Hill is also the start of the Lyke Wake Walk. Ahead are the moors of Carlton and Cringle.

113. On the way down to Scarth Nick the first real sight of Cleveland can be enjoyed. It is a fine moment. To the right Carlton Moor rises into eminence while in the distance between it and the shapely outlier of Whorle Hill is Easby Moor and Captain Cook's 'pike'. But it is to the abrupt conical shape to the left of Whorle Hill that the eye is drawn. This is Roseberry Topping whose conspicuous form will refuse to be ignored for many hours and many miles!

114. Signs informative and warning near Coalmire.

115. The path through Coalmire.

116. and later approaching Scugdale.

117. The wicket gate leading the 'way' down to the beck.

118. The ford near Hollin Hill Farm.

119. Scugdale. Having crossed the road there is time to exchange some sunny morning pleasantries with the council workmen. The opportunity is also used to roll some tobacco and recharge the briar. Behind the tractor is Near Moor which the Cleveland Way has following at its foot.

120. Scugdale. One of the spoil tips left by the iron miners in the last century.

121. A look back at the sharp climb onto Live Moor.

122. Live Moor boundary stone.

123. Live Moor. The path winds on eastwards.

124. The scraped and scoured surface of Carlton Moor with its windsock for the gliders.

125. The wild edge of Carlton Moor looking west.

126. Ancient and modern on Carlton Moor summit. Cringle Moor lies ahead and the path can be seen making its snaking climb.

127. A view over the old workings on Carlton Moor to the Cleveland escarpment and Roseberry Topping.

128. From the Moor the path descends to Carlton Bank where the road between Carlton and Chop Gate climbs into the moors.

129. The stone seat and 'Toposcope' on Cringle Moor.

130. Looking back to Carlton Moor from the same spot.

131. The scene to the east introduces Cold Moor and Hasty Bank. Beyond is the main Cleveland escarpment now looking appreciably nearer.

132. From the stone seat on Cringle End the Cleveland Way turns into the moor to reach the 1400 ft (427 m) contour above Kirby bank.

133. Stony message beside the path. Surely not an advertisement for British Rail!!

134. A look back at Cringle End from the top of Kirby Bank.

135. Moorland sheep and Cringle Moor. Alive on the top.

136. Dead at the bottom.

137. Before making the assault on Cold Moor a study of Cringle Moor shows the line of spoil from old alum and jet workings which roughly mark out the 900 foot contour.

138. A breath-taking pause on the way up Cold Moor at a crossing of ancient tracks.

139. Cringle Moor from Cold Moor.

140. Next comes Hasty Bank after the usual bone creaking descent!

141. The Waintstone greeting on the top of Hasty Bank can add either to the pleasure or the irritation!

142. Ravenscar or the scarp edge of Hasty Bank. The Cleveland Way can be traced climbing to the right of the plantation on the next moor which as the Carr Ridge is the first stage of the journey on to Urra Moor.

143. A picture to the south takes in Bilsdale with the road to Helmsley just visible. The persistent image of the 1000 foot television mast on Bilsdale West Moor is still very much with us!

144. At the foot of Hasty Bank the path crosses the Stokesley — Helmsley road when the traffic allows. Roseberry Topping is still there looking steadily more arrogant.

145. The 'grind' up from the road at Haggs Gate.

146. Wall company.

147. Stile entry to Urra Moor. The view back to Hasty Bank.

148. The narrow rock-strewn gorge leading onto Carr Ridge.

149. Entry to the solitude of Urra Moor under threatening skies.

150. With the path now on its way round to the main Cleveland escarpment this is a suitable moment to take note of the one-time Ingleby railway Incline which is well seen in this picture rising up its gradient of 1 in 5 onto Greenhow Moor.

151. Wordy warnings on Urra Moor.

152. The gentle but stony rise to the peak at Botton Head.

153. Summit Trig Point on Botton Head marking a height of 1490 feet (454m) — the highest point on the whole walk.

154. The 'Hand stone' sign post on Botton Head dating from 1711.

155. On the trackbed of the former Rosedale ironstone railway at Bloworth Crossing. Here the Lyke Wake Walk continues on through the gate and across the moors to the coast. The Cleveland Way, however, performs a 'V' turn and takes the road along the main escarpment of Greenhow Moor.

Some idea of a change in the weather is perhaps evident in this picture and of course it had to come on the most exposed and isolated part of the walk!

156. Following a most violent electric storm with percussion and stair-rod accompaniment a look back from near 'Jenny Bradley' finds a young Walker soaked through and with water-filled boots squelching along a path that has become a temporary stream.

157. Jenny Bradley and the two boundary stones.

158. No 7 shooting butt and beyond it the familiar profiles of old moor acquaintances.

159. The path rising gently up to Burton Howe

160. Drifting down towards Kildale from Tidy Brown Hill.

161. Gate retrospect near Battersby Bank.

162. Curlews on the wing away to the east vocally celebrate
an end to the thundery demonstration.

163. A somewhat wet woolly group find themselves undergoing
a bit of droving on the rise over Battersby Bank.

164. Juniper Gate where the Cleveland Way takes up the motor road from Baysdale Abbey to Kildale.

165. Torn and disturbed skies collect over the western moors. A late evening photograph taken from near Park House Farm near Kildale.

166. Turn right for Kildale village.

167. Kildale approach.

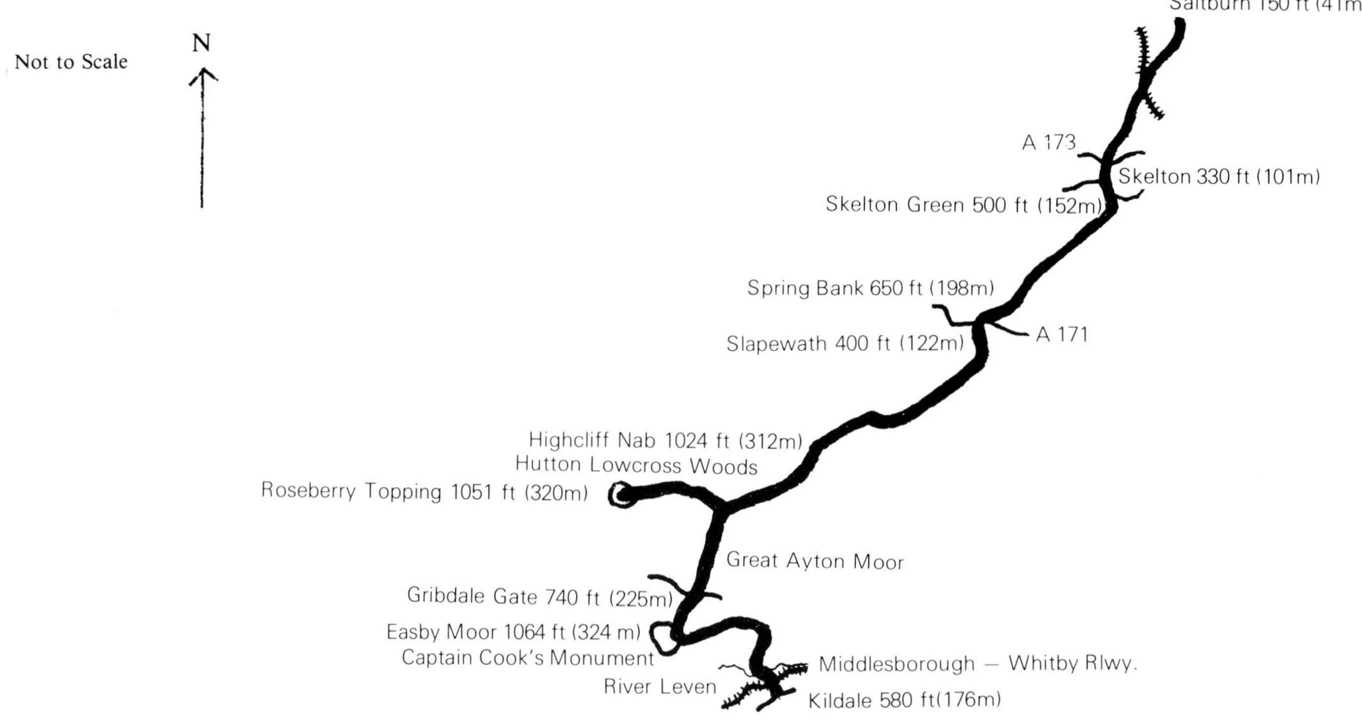

Kildale to Saltburn

KILDALE — SALTBURN
14 miles (22.5 km)

The lift out of the Leven valley in Kildale takes the path up a metalled road to the brow of Pale End Plantation where it turns west along a forest ride onto Easby Moor. The trees here give way to an open bracken-covered moor dominated by the monument to Captain Cook which looks out over the plain. The 'way' then heads northwards again dropping down to Gribdale Gate to cross the igneous intrusion known as the Cleveland Dyke.

Climbing alongside a wall onto Ayton Bank, the physical presence of Roseberry Topping is now very close at hand. Like the Kilburn White Horse, Roseberry Topping is an optional extra but it cannot be ignored! A breath demanding scramble up its steep east side is amply repaid on the top when, standing on the huge slabs and blocks of sandstone, one finds oneself looking over a sheer drop of 60 feet or more to a mound of rocky rubble below. Presumably this once formed the hill's western face before its collapse in 1907 due to mining activity below. The view from the top of Roseberry is a special one taking in not only the familiar territory of the western moors, the Pennines and the plain but also large areas of industrial Tees-side, its river and a considerable expanse of sea to the east.

Retracing the steps back to the gate on Roseberry Common the 'way' continues eastwards over the shoulder of Newton Moor, skirts the hanging woods above Hutton Lowcross, and then follows a sheep track through the heather to a patch of marsh in the Codhill valley. This leads onto Highcliffe Nab, another prominent moor standing guard over the ancient town of Guisborough now a Tees-side dormitory.

From Highcliffe it is back into woodland as the path wanders slowly down to the main road crossing at Slapewath Bridge where once again water, road and the erstwhile railway utilised the gap through the moors.

The last stages of the approach to Slapewath are decidedly scrappy but significantly so. Inroads seem to have been made into the valley sides at numerous places at different times and spoil tips are scattered about in ugly profusion. Among the more overgrown ones there stands the gaunt remains of buildings and tall chimneys suggesting evidence of a one time conversion of heat energy into mechanical power.

Such remains are but a sample of several that are to be found all along the lower slopes of the moors we have just walked right back to Roseberry Topping. Most of them bear silent witness to the great Cleveland ironstone era when these hills disgorged their ore by the thousand tons to feed both local and distant bloomeries and furnaces. The names of the mines were household words to iron and steel men a century ago — Hutton, Belmont, South Belmont, Spa Wood and Slapewath.

The provision of a pub called the 'Fox & Hounds' at Slapewath Bridge is a very thoughtful gesture and as the route actually passes its doors a wayfarer would not be displaying any undue weakness if he sought rest and refreshment at an hour of licence. Whatever the fancy the next task is to tackle the rise onto Spring Bank which is made via the quarry rim beside the busy Middlesbrough — Whitby main road.

Once on the top, the route skirts first a plantation and then pastures and crops until it joins an increasingly defined track leading to Airy Hill Farm beyond which the road is 'made-up' through to Skelton Green. Skelton with its satelites of Skelton Green, New Skelton and North Skelton was a mining village until the last of the iron ore mines at North Skelton closed in 1964, and its intermittent rows of terraced houses rise and fall with the restless contours. The Cleveland Way crosses Skelton's main shopping street to find an exit past the library, the police station and a new estate of houses. A well used field path then leads one decisively towards the line of trees ahead called Thorny Hill Wood and beyond them, (as has been apparent for several miles,) lies Saltburn, the sea, and, maybe, a well earned rest.

It all seems so easy now that the wayfarer is an easy prey for Fate who attends him as he enters the wood. He finds the ground falling steeply down into a deep gorge cut by the Skelton Beck. Crossing the beck and passing beneath the arches of an enormous railway viaduct the gradient is then fiercely upwards again through the shaded poles of timber and no small effort is required to drag the legs up onto Saltburn's street level.

Saltburn is very much a product of the second Iron Age. It was built as a resort during the 19th century by ironmasters like Henry Pease of Darlington and its grid-like plan with the shared grandeurs of its neo-gothic parish church and its once railway-owned and served Zetland Hotel pre-eminent, makes an interesting study in Victorian coastal town design.

168. Kildale. The bridge over the River Leven.

169. The lift out of Kildale to Pale End Plantation. This evening shot looks back to Bankside Farm beyond the gate and to Kildale's church. After a long period of fierce heat the recent storm is showing some effects as the vapours rise in the cooling air leaving only the tops of the moors visible above them.

170. The top of Pale End Brow where the 'way' turns west into the plantation.

171. Forest walk along Coate Moor ridge with fly fellow travellers!

172. Leaving the cover of the trees on Easby Moor is to discover our friend Roseberry Topping looking decidedly aggressive as it awaits the attentions of the wayfarer.

173. Looking across the valley of Loundsdale Beck to Great Ayton Moor. The gap divides two conifer plantations. Pine on the left and spruce on the right.

174. Captain Cook's monument on Easby Moor.

175. Plaque tribute to a local boy who made good.

176. The view south west from the monument looks across to those familiar characters which read from left to right — Cold, Cringle, Carlton, Live and Near moors.

177. Gribdale Gate where the path crosses the volcanic Cleveland Dyke.

178. Wall studies on Ayton Bank.

179. Collapsed boundary stone on Black Bank.

180. Gate on Newton Moor giving access to Roseberry Topping.

181. View from near the summit of Roseberry Topping looking across to Easby Moor and Captain Cook's monument.

182. Mining and subsidence have always maintained a close cause and effect relationship and Roseberry Topping offers a sensational example of this. Following years of ironstone extraction from beneath the hill the west face collapsed in 1907. Now, considerable care is needed when approaching the edge where a sheer drop of nearly 70 feet presents itself. From between the huge blocks of sandstone on the top the view to the north towards Teesside is somewhat obscured by heat haze.

183. A photograph over the western edge looks down onto the rock debris below and catches a sea gull obviously enjoying a gliding holiday among the air currents as a change from the north sea breezes on the coast.

184. The view south west from near the trig point shows the moors west of Carlton and also an interesting close up of the bedded sandstone.

185. A final view to the north west picks up the fringes of residential Tees-side.

186. A contemplative reappraisal of Roseberry Topping after a rather undignified descent.

87. Returning to the main route on Newton Moor an examination of the landscape back through the gate finds the vapours and fumes of industry rising from Tees-side.

188. The next summit on the route. Eastwards across Hutton Moor rises Highcliff Nab.

189. Approaching the rough Hutton Gate to Percy Cross road,

190. Robust growth in Hutton Lowcroft Woods.

191. Rut and boulder gateway.

192. An acorn and brick arrow invitation to a stretch of undefined 'way'
near Guisborough Moor.

193. Sheep track through the heather leads the way to the Codh

194 Approaching the Codhill dip.

195. Marsh, 'mush' and pond weed in the Codhill Slack gathering grounds.

196. 'Coke' tin polution near Codhill slack.

197. Dumbledoor beetle with sheep droppings a little further on.

198. Interested camera-conscious onlooker near Highcliff.

199. Highcliff. Wicket gate and acorn sign.

200. In the oak wood behind Highcliff Nab.

201. The covered way to the scarp edge.

202. The rock face of the nab with Guisborough below.

203. Guisborough from the edge — a study in dormitary growth. Behind the town are the detached hills around Upleatham and beyond obscured by the heat haze is the sea.

204. A view back to Highcliff edge takes in Hutton Hall and the south western fringes of Guisborough. Eston Moor at the back effectively blocks out the view of Middlesborough and Tees-side.

205. Nearly three miles of forest rides have to be followed before the 'over-spill' gap at Slapewath is reached. Here, beyond Spring Wood a look back finds Highcliff still very much in sight.

206. Unofficial acorn sign and arrow on a wayside stone.

207. Magic circle nearby.

208. Ahead the plantation ride perspective emphasises the shape of Warsett Hill on the coast which the Cleveland Way will pass on Hunt Cliff.

209. A strange collection of dead timber on the way down to Slapewath.

210. Stile at the bottom of Justice bank showing both vertical and horizontal acorn symbols. The latter are no doubt intended for those who are on their knees!

211. Branch and bracken obstructions near Spa Wood.

212. Slapewath dominated by its pub — the Fox and Hounds. Spring Bank rises at the back of it and beside the spoil tips nearer the camera runs the beck. Glimpses of tall chimneys and spoil heaps in the landscape speak of the great iron mining days of the last century when this whole area was bursting with activity.

213. Another industrial relic. The remains of the drift mine at Spa Wood.

214. Hostile spiked natural obstruction to be avoided on the way down to the main road.

215. Tip begets tip. A recent addition to the mine tips.

216. Broom seed pod presentation nearby.

217. The A171 main road.

218. Entrance to Slapewath quarry where the alum shale heaps are being removed for use on building sites.

219. The Fox and Hounds from the climb onto Sring Bank.

220. Another shot taken from the top of Spring Bank looking down onto the quarry and the coach cluttered main road.

221. Stile on the top of Spring Bank and a last look at those enormous tips.

222. A peer through the trees to the north.

223. Airy Hill Farm.

224. Power Lines near Cripple Hill. An apt name, maybe?!

225. Skelton Green approach. Beyond is the line of moors ending in Warsett Hill and Hunt Cliff.

226. Skelton Green. Pigeon baskets.

227. Public footpath across to Skelton.

228. Downhill to Skelton. Beyond it crowned by its church tower is Saltburn and the mist concealed sea.

229. Skelton. Derwentwater Road. A rare moment of suburban delight complete with lamp post acorn and police station.

230. Some more recent building achievements on the way through Skelton.

231. Skelton exit. The end of road walking and the beginning of a restricted footpath. Warsett Hill rises behind the notice.

232. Footpath across to Thorny Close Wood.

233. North Eastern Railwayana. The splendid viaduct over the Skelton Beck.

234. The beck itself running under leafy shadow.

235. Deadwood fungus on the weary climb up through Riftswood.

236. Saltburn street level. A look back at the path rising from the depths.

237. Saltburn. Straight ahead for the prom and a right turn for Whitby. On the left is a dignified row of period, five storey hotels with Mansard roof covering.

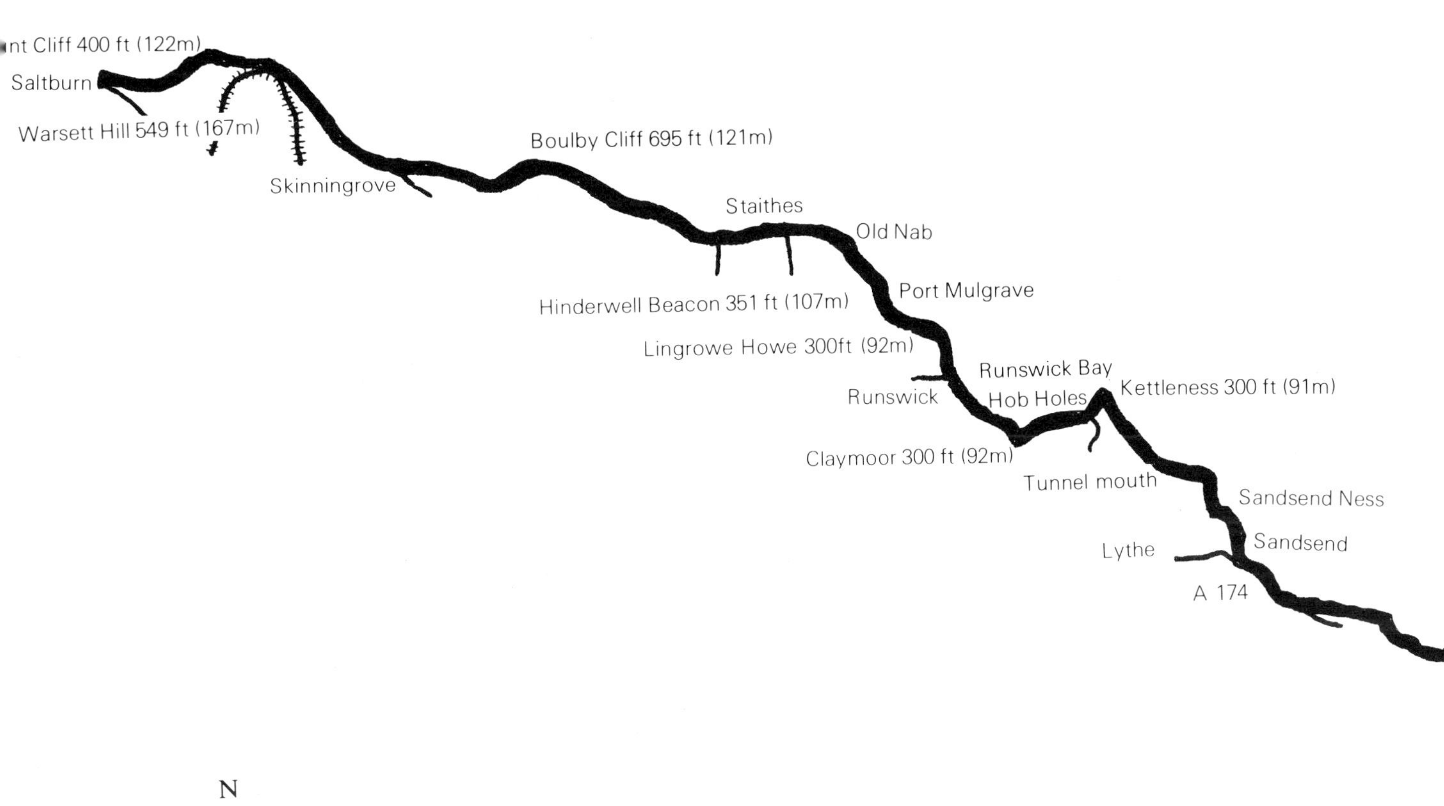

nt Cliff 400 ft (122m)
Saltburn
Warsett Hill 549 ft (167m)
Skinningrove
Boulby Cliff 695 ft (121m)
Staithes
Old Nab
Hinderwell Beacon 351 ft (107m)
Port Mulgrave
Lingrowe Howe 300ft (92m)
Runswick Bay
Runswick
Hob Holes
Kettleness 300 ft (91m)
Claymoor 300 ft (92m)
Tunnel mouth
Sandsend Ness
Lythe
Sandsend
A 174
Whitby
N
Not to Scale
Saltburn to Whitby

SALTBURN TO WHITBY
19 miles (30 km)

Saltburn is more than a turning point on the Cleveland Way. It ushers in a completely fresh experience. For the next 45 miles the sea will exert its power both as a force in shaping the landscape and as an attraction for humanity who seek its proximity for work and pleasure.

As a stretch of cliff coastline it has few rivals and from now on headland follows bay, or nab and ness follows wyke in recurring succession.

The 'way' strikes off from Saltburn on a morbid note when having left the good-life hotels on the high promenade it passes a grim little building labelled MORTUARY. Such a cautionary start is not entirely inappropriate, however, because another few yards brings the path onto an unfenced cliff edge where a careless step would no doubt provide another candidate for the mortuary. It is well to remember that these sea cliffs are under relentless attack from the elements and are undergoing constant change.

As the path gains height and approaches Huntcliff a keen scrutiny of the western horizon on a clear day should produce some farewell sights of our old friend Roseberry Topping now much diminished by distance but still looking decidedly unrepentant. Huntcliff also brings the return of the railway that the walker passed beneath while grovelling under the viaduct in the depths of Skelton Beck. It approaches the cliff edge from the west and after rounding Warsett Hill disappears westwards again towards Carlin How. Now reduced to single line mineral status and terminating at Boulby potash mine it is sadly all that remains of the one time Scarborough-Middlesbrough line — one of the most beautiful coastal railways in Britain.

Ahead now the chimneys and rooftops of industry mark the position of Skinningrove which is reached either by a slimey descent down a cliff of boulder clay to the beach below or down a slag-tip cliff nearer the works. The latter is preferable.

Skinningrove is an astonishing place. Set in an exquisite valley where some of the richest and thickest Cleveland ironstone deposits were discovered and mined, this iron, steel and mining community grew up beside Kilton Beck beneath the shadow of its own works on the cliff above. So searing is the conflict between the landscape and industry that the place possesses a compelling 'beauty' that beggars description.

The mines up the valley have, of course, now closed though their tips are still visible from the coast. Also, iron and steel making are no longer carried on, so that large parts of the works have been dismantled leaving only the rolling mill as a reminder of a proud industrial past.

Skinningrove village is built in the valley bottom and its depressing collection of terraces serve to underline the 19th century exploitation of Nature both as landscape and people. Those who mined the ore or made the steel were accorded conditions very different from those who owned and directed the enterprises. But if their living conditions were sometimes cramped the people of Skinningrove like those of many an industrial village became welded into a wonderfully strong community and this spirit still survives as the bureaucracy which recently tried to rehouse them elsewhere discovered. The village recognises the inherent value of its position by the sea and it is not prepared to relinquish it to the builders of well appointed 'High Class' sea-front residences and who blames them?

After this remarkable lesson in industrial history the Cleveland Way makes a sharp climb up the valley side above the village and as the path rises higher and higher over Hummersea bank the anticipations become concentrated upon the challenge of Boulby cliff which rises solidly ahead with its stepped profile.

Boulby's eminence has not deterred man's attentions. Far from it. The cliff has been heavily raided for alum, jet, iron ore, building stone and even coal with the result that the whole shape of the cliff has been considerably altered. Evidence of the various operations is strewn around in tips, holes and in the vestiges of buildings.

The path passes quite close to the 699 foot summit of Boulby at Rockcliffe Beacon after which it drifts down past Boulby hamlet to pick up the tarmac road leading down into Staithes. Away to the west beyond the main road the tall concrete chimney of Boulby potash mine proclaims North Yorkshire's newest industry.

At the risk of adding to the tourist population it has to be admitted that Staithes is a gem. Tucked into the narrow gorge where Roxby Beck flows out into the sea below Cowbar Nab it is still essentially a fishing village of narrow cobbled streets whose character is at once one of antipathy to the motor car. Its growth is one that requires only the physical involvement of people and not their machines, and like some other settlements along this coast parts of it have a reputation for disappearing into the sea. Its sea-front pub, the 'Cod & Lobster' is one such building being the third hostelry of that name to be erected on the site!

The exit from Staithes is up Church Street from where the path takes to the fields before returning to the cliff edge for the rise to Hinderwell Beacon. After this the 'way' curves high above the one-time harbour of Port Mulgrave where ironstone from the inland Grinkle mines was brought out by narrow gauge tunnel and track to be shipped round to the Tees for smelting.

Keeping above the Rosedale cliffs the wayfarer follows the shallow bay past another neolithic long barrow. He then leaves the cliff top abruptly and is directed inland along a field path to the motor road at the top of Runswick bank. Runswick is another delightful motor-non-grata village at the bottom of a steep cliff with fine views over the bay to Kettleness. The Cleveland Way drops down through the village to the beach and taking to the sand it follows the cliffs as far as Hob Holes where the Claymoor Beck drains into the sea.

As suggested by its name the clamber onto Claymoor is not achieved without some slithery hazards in wet weather and it is a relief to reach the top again and follow Highcliffe and Whitestones cliff round the bay to the headland at Kettleness. A row of Coastguard cottages, the old station house and a few huddled dwellings are all that is left of the mining hamlet of Kettleness. Its older properties near the foot of the cliffs were swept into the sea by a landslide in 1829.

Rounding Lucky Dog's Point a conspicuous inland landmark comes into view in the form of Lythe parish church. The church is detached from the village and its short spire is a landmark for many miles around. Also ahead in clear conditions are the sea-front buildings at Whitby with the abbey ruins prominent amongst them.

At Stonecliff End the path does a brief switch back to find a hole in the hawthorn bushes where a flight of rather treacherous steps takes it steeply down onto the course of the former coast railway which appeared earlier and has never been far away from the path since Staithes. The line here came out of the 1657 yard long Sandsend Tunnel whose closeness to the cliff edge at its north western end must have been a factor in its closure. Coastal railways are expensive to maintain and cliff sections like those we have walked are very prone to shifts and collapses.

In some places it is now difficult to realise that trains ever travelled over this ground because the erosion and movement of the cliffs have twisted the trackbed out of all recognition. Indeed in some places the course of the line is now on the point of disappearing over the edge.

The trackbed from the tunnel is pleasant walking and it takes the walker past the relics of some vigorous workings where alum and jet were once extracted leaving impressive tunnels, quarries and mounds of spoil scattered about.

Sandsend sees the beginning of a broad sandy beach extending through to Whitby. The Cleveland Way is officially routed along the main road but a better choice is the beach below it and this can be used all the way to Whitby where numerous steps, slopes and paths give access to the golf course or the promenade.

Divided by the River Esk, Whitby is a port and town with an illustrious history as is still evident in many of its older streets and buildings. However, the medieval intimacy of the old town which was not harmed by the arrival of the railway or by the development of its promenade and hotel 'suburb' does now seem to be under some threat and once again it is the tyrannical demands of road transport which causes corners to be widened here and the odd building to be demolished there. Indeed, Whitby at the moment seems to be struggling hard to find an image to satisfy modern tourism and it would be a disaster if it were to deny its past because its history has always been a major attraction. It needs to be clear about the clientele it wishes to attract because it has too many rivals for it to offer itself as a resort for everyman.

Among its undoubted blessings are a splendid harbour and fish dock, good beaches, a fine abbey ruin and cliff-top parish church, a goodly range of shops and cafes including some appropriate examples of the fish and chip variety and, (worthy of special mention), a locally flavoured museum which delights in its organised chaos.

On the debit side must be mentioned quite the most anti-social colony of gulls imaginable not only for their unhygienic demonstrations of Newton's law but also for their round-the-clock vocal bombardment. During the day one gladly accepts the mocking calls of gulls as an essential part of sea-siding but at 3am it is a different matter and any benevolent feelings one might have felt towards them twelve hours earlier rapidly disappear.

The author vividly remembers glowering from his hotel window during the small hours as he analysed the situation with the aid of the street lamps. Each rooftop supported its own tired community which showed every sign of trying to sleep until a rogue group of agents provocateurs winging round above the town in rabble formation dived upon them uttering screeches of derision and invective. One roosting gathering after another was scattered amid the most vociferous clammer, after which they would noisily recover a perch and attempt sleep once more until of course the agitators returned again.

The notoriety of Whitby's seagulls is not a local matter. Following a mention on a morning news broadcast their reputation became a cause of national concern. So, wayfarer, if you are contemplating a night in the town, (as of course you should) be warned!

238. Saltburn departure down the slope.

239. No parking in front of the morgue.

240. The cliff path and the first of the red-letter warnings!

241. Saltburn retrospect. On the left is the famous Zetland Hotel.

242. In thickening weather a keen scrutiny of the south western horizon picks out a last sight of an auld acquaintance that will not be forgot. Roseberry Topping, no less, together with its neighbours Hutton Moor and Highcliff.

243. A barley crop nodding encouragement beside the path.

244. The way ahead to Hunt Cliff.

245. A further Saltburn retrospect. Behind is Upleatham hill and on the rain obscured horizon the faint shapes of Teessmouth industry can be discerned.

246. Hunt Cliff approach while beyond Boulby cliff 'noses' into view.

247. Another nosey greeting through the fence.

248. A 'tailly' insult further on!

249. The railway on Hunt Cliff coincides with the appearance of the chimneys of Skinningrove.

250. The jetty at Skinningrove and the mass of Boulby cliff have their forms softened by the arrival of heavy rain.

251. Dirty weather for the crossing of the boulder clay topped cliffs leading to Skinningrove.

52. On the delightful beach of Cattersty Sands. The cliffs ahead are capped with slag from the works.

253. Sand and limpet shells.

254. Sand ripple patterns.

255. Wavelet patterns.

256. Slag boulders below the works cliff.

257. Slag scarp.

258. From the steel works jetty a study of Hummersea cliff and Boulby.

259. Skinningrove. Steel work force terrace.

260. Mrs Sally Leist of No. 9 Stone Row. "I'm going up 91 you know and I'm the oldest person in the village. I can remember when we had five furnaces on blast here.".

261. Two more local residents both wearing eyes of suspicion.

263. A retrospective contemplation of Skinningrove and its works. The latter has now lost much of its vigorous industrial character owing to progressive demolition which is still under way. At one time the cintering plant, bloomeries and furnaces extended right along to the cliff edge. The decorated lofts of the numerous pigeon fanciers scattered up the valley sides above the village symbolise a very strong local sport, which has an enormous following and tradition in the village.

264. A photograph from the same position looking south up the Kilton Beck valley to the local mines which once supplied ore for the works. Their tips and heaps remain as silent witnesses of a past era.

265. On the way up to Hummersea cliff a view back over the Skinningrove jetty to Hunt cliff and Warsett Hill. In the foreground a wartime gun position still guards the coastal approaches beside a fine display of coltsfoot.

266. Hummersea Cliff.

267. The way ahead to Warren Cottages.

268. Gaining height. Another look back.

269. Boulby cliff approach. Climbing up to the top 'step'.

270. Boulby cliff. Yet another retrospect affords an appreciation of the cliff's geological structure. Below the covering of Lower Estuarine Sandstone is a layer of weak coal followed by another thin bed of sandstone called the Dogger. The strata then descends into the Lower Jurassic sequence which includes the Upper Lias ironstone, alum shales, Jet rock, the Middle Lias Cleveland Ironstone and finally the shales and sandstones of the Lower lias.

271. Boulby Cliff. This photograph gives some idea of the extent of successive 'plunderings' of alum, jet, iron, building stone and even coal. Ahead lies Cowbar Nab and Staithes.

272. The remarkable spectacles on the seaward side should not be allowed to detract from the fine airy vistas to the south west where the high moortops around Danby raise themselves into prominence.

273. Also inland the police radio mast near Rockcliff
Beacon which marks Boulby's summit.

274. Boulby Cliff.

275. A short stretch of high weed 'jungle' to cross before the down grade begins.

276. On the way down to Boulby hamlet. The Staithes village 'overspill' is apparent below Hinderwell Beacon which is the next rise to come.

278. Boulby watch dog.

277. Approach to Boulby.

279. A recent chapter in North Yorkshire's industrial saga. Boulby potash mine.

280. Lions couchant and watching on gate guard duty near Boulby.

281. Entry to Staithes along Cowbar Lane.

282. A look at the east side of Boulby cliff from Cowbar Lane.

283. Staithes — a tourist dream village. Dropping down the slope to the bridge over Staithes Beck. Not a car in sight!

284. Lazy watchers in Staithes.

285. Staithes. Boats on the beck and lobster pots on the quay.

286. Coast path sign on the sea front.

287. A breath recovery photograph after a hearty meal looks back over Staithes as the path rises once more to the cliff top.

288. Keeping close to the cliff edge as the ground rises this shot looks back onto Old Nab.

289. Another retrospect from near Hinderwell Beacon takes a long hard look at Boulby and its potash mine chimneys on the left. The settlement of Staithes Lane End is prominent ahead.

290. The scene westwards towards Borrowby.

291. Coastline anticipation. Seen from above Port Mulgrave the headland of Lingrow juts out into the sea to form the west point of Runswick Bay. On the far side is Kettleness which even from this distance has clearly been much quarried and disturbed.

292. Port Mulgrave — another piece of industrial history. It was here in the last century that a mile long narrow gauge railway tunnel emerged bringing iron ore for shipment to Tees and Tyneside from the Grinkle mines 2½ miles inland.

293. On the way to Runswick Bay — the path near Lingrow.

4. The sharp right turn which directs the Cleveland Way from the cliff edge to the motor road at the top of Runswick Bank. A steep and treacherous descent is thus avoided.

295.

The pub and cross roads at Runswick Bank top. The route here turns left for the village.

296. Downhill to Runswick.

297. Runswick village. Sea front, lifeboat station and high class residences.

298. Runswick Bay — beach images.

299. Runswick Bay — more ripple patterns.

300. The beach exit at Hob Holes. Note the boulder clay covering of the cliffs.

301. The return to the tops up Claymore Beck.

302 This view from near the top looks back down the path.

303. Runswick retrospect.

304. Approaching Catbeck Hill Cliff. Beyond is the 'mauled' shape of Kettleness Point.

305. Kettleness. Surviving and additional dwellings of a former jet mining hamlet that fell into the sea in 1829.

306. Kettleness. Coast path signpost and competing parsley permit a view back over Runswick Bay.

307. Rape of a headland. The contorted contours of dumps, heaps and tips left by the jet miners.

8.
e first distant sight of Whitby. The cliff promontory ahead is Keldhowe Point.

309.
The north end of Kettleness tunnel through which the coast railway once ran.

310. Keldhowe Point.

311. A conspicuous landmark for many miles is Lythe's parish church which stands aloof from its village on the top of the bank leading down to Sandsend. The farm ahead is Overdale.

312. A close-up of Keldhowe Point shows the ledge where the line of the original coast railway of the Whitby, Redcar and Middlesborough Union Company was engineered. A short tunnel took it through the headland, and this still remains. Perhaps not surprisingly the exposed earthworks collapsed into the sea before its completion hence the new course later adopted further west.

313. A retrospect from Keldhowe Point.

314. Whitby lit by a late westering sun.

315. Harvest sculptures near Deepgrove Farm.

316. The 'black hole' of Stonecliff where some very irregular and difficult steps take the Cleveland Way down onto the abandoned trackbed of the coast railway.

318. The south east portal of the 1675 foot long Sandsend tunnel.

319. Trackbed path.

320. The extensive alum quarry near Deepgrove where the workings were on a massive scale.

321. Sandsend Ness whose whole physical profile has been disturbed by the extraction of alum and jet.

322. Sandsend approach.

323. 324. Pathside pollen plunderers.

325. The path near Sandsend. The course of the railway is so contorted here that it is difficult to realise now that trains ever travelled this stretch.

326. Looking down onto the wave cut rock platform near Sandsend.

327. The old Sandsend station.

328. The steps to the beach.

329. Sandsend sea front.

330. From a path up from the beach to Whitby a backward look to Sandsend Ness and Keldhowe Point.

331. Arrival at Whitby's hotel quarter dominated by the Metropole Hotel on the right.

332. Whitby. Holiday making.

3. Gothic composition utilising the whalebone
arch and Whitby Abbey.

334. Whitby. Distributing the confectionary beneath the gaze of Captain Cook.

335. Whitby fish quay.

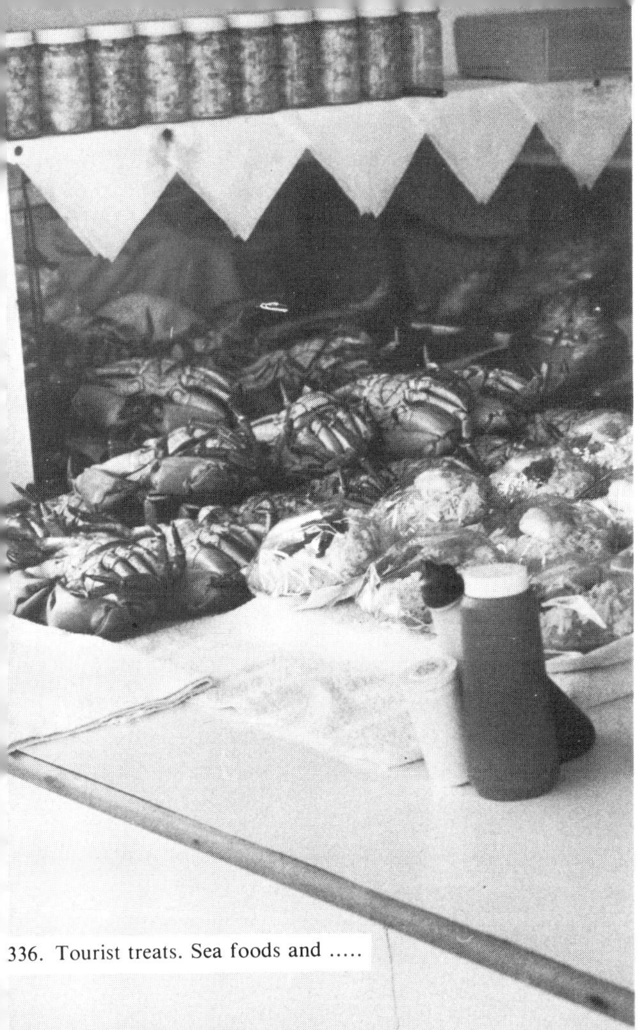

336. Tourist treats. Sea foods and .....

337. Sweetmeats.

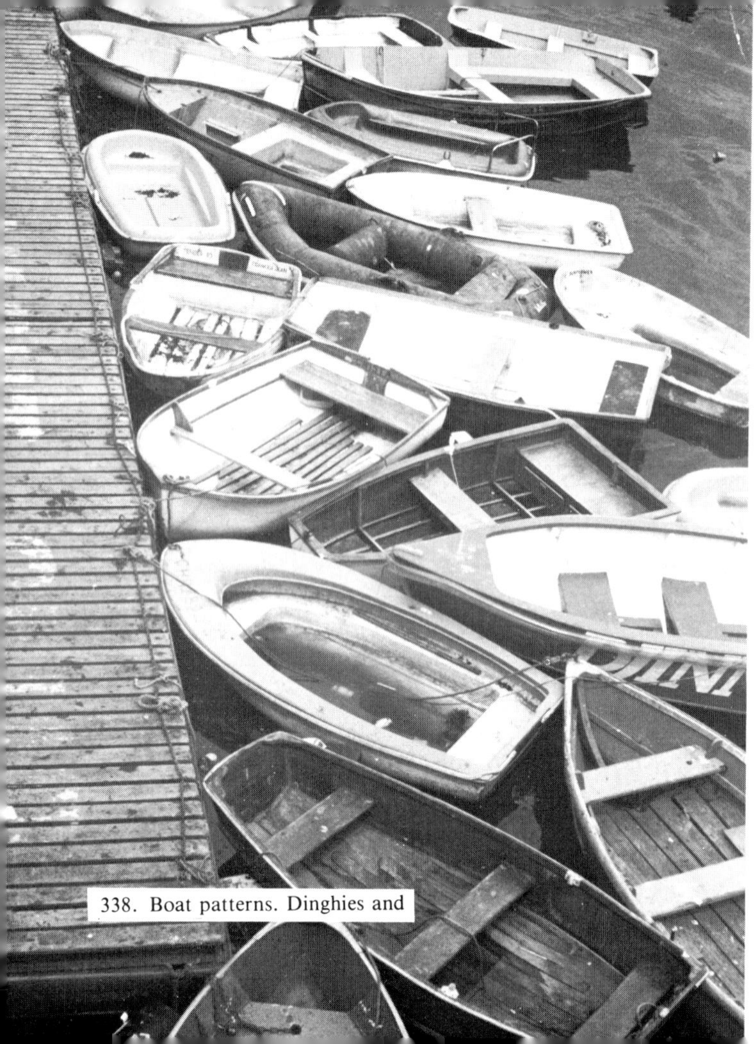

338. Boat patterns. Dinghies and

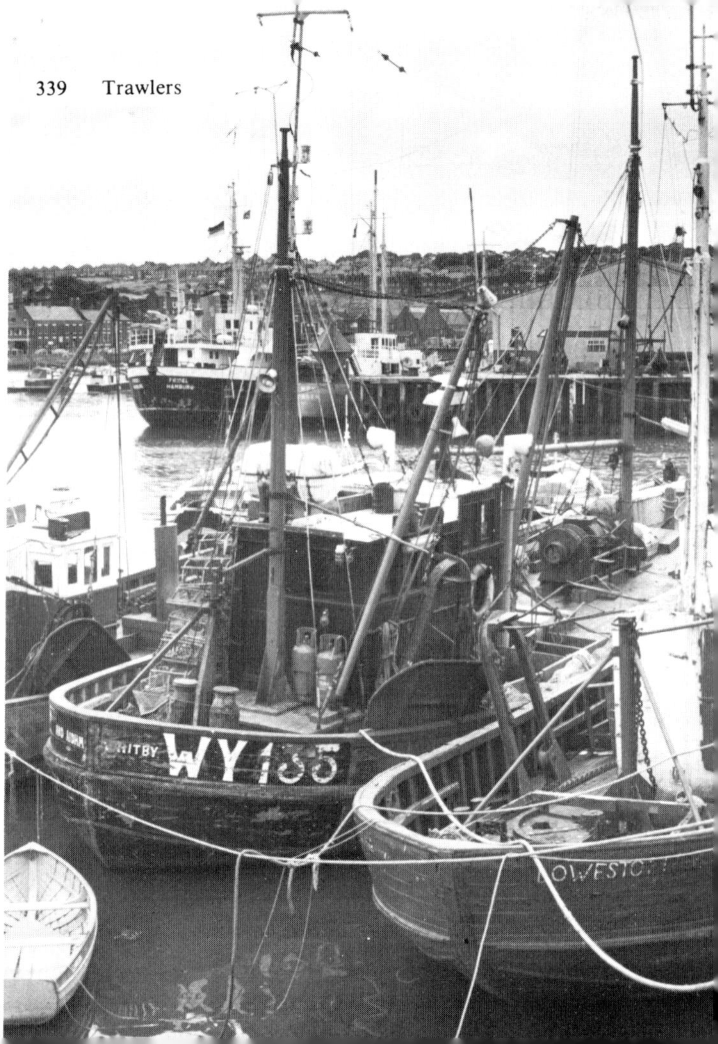

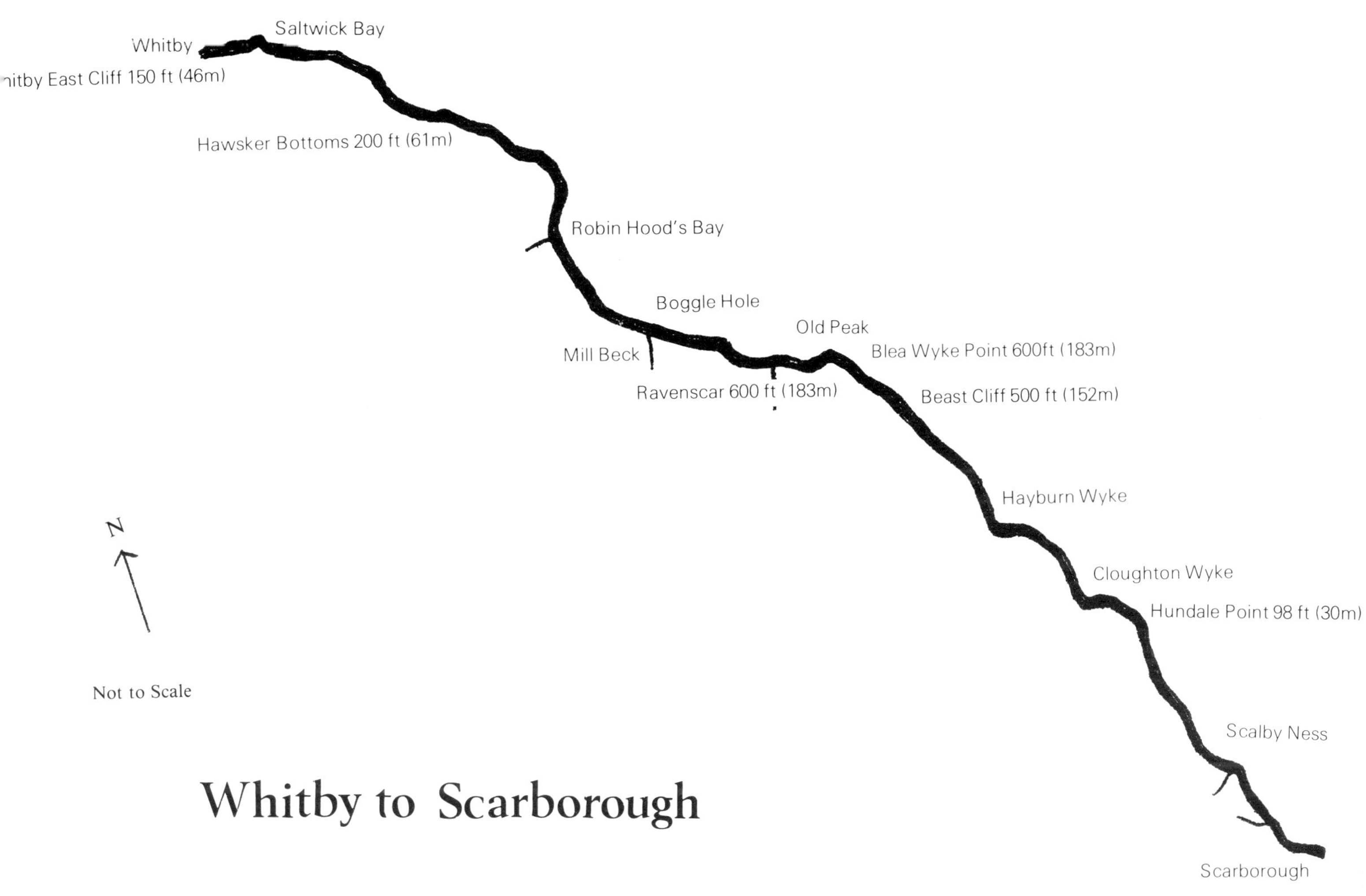

Whitby
Saltwick Bay
Whitby East Cliff 150 ft (46m)
Hawsker Bottoms 200 ft (61m)
Robin Hood's Bay
Boggle Hole
Old Peak
Mill Beck
Blea Wyke Point 600ft (183m)
Ravenscar 600 ft (183m)
Beast Cliff 500 ft (152m)
Hayburn Wyke
Cloughton Wyke
Hundale Point 98 ft (30m)
Scalby Ness
Scarborough
N
Not to Scale
Whitby to Scarborough

WHITBY TO SCARBOROUGH
19 miles (30 km)

199 steps or a gradient of 1 in 3 is the price of resuming the walk to Scarborough. It also brings the walker onto Whitby's east cliff beside the old parish church, past the coastguard cottages and the distinguished ruins of the Benedictine abbey of St. Hilda with its lancet rhythms of solid and space.

From the cliff top a popular path leads the 'way' across to the caravan park above Saltwick Bay and then back to the edge for a close look at the coastguard's fog warning hooter known locally, because of its vocal accomplishment, as the Whitby "Bull".

The coastline now turns steadily south eastwards until on drawing near to Ness Point the fine sweep of Robin Hood's Bay opens out ahead ending with a flourish at Old Peak, the high cliff above Ravenscar.

The route into the village of Robin Hood's Bay brings with it a sight of the substantial concrete coastal defences that have been required for the security of the old village and also a return once more of the coast railway trackbed which partners the walker into the resort.

Robin Hood's Bay possesses a dual personality. The early sea-threatened settlement is tightly clustered above the sea front like Staithes and Runswick while the later 'graft' has spread behind it on the cliff top.

In order to do its job properly the Cleveland Way has to go down into the old village, of course, and a pleasant experience it is to wander 'with the brakes on' down through such delightfully organic dwellings. The ascent again from beach level takes the path through a steep alleyway onto Cowfield Hill from where it follows the cliff tops along the bay to the gully called Boggle Hole which requires some cautious negotiation.

Crossing the Mill Beck beside the Youth Hostel the path then recovers height only to grovel into another gully a short distance further on, this time over the Stoupe Beck. The way out of this is up a brief length of road and once back on top a cliff-top path takes over until the route turns inland towards Brow side Farm to pick up a winding track leading up into Ravenscar.

The moor to the south west beyond Stoupe Brow above the 'way' is a remarkable piece of no-man's land. It is littered with tumuli, earthworks and stones of ancient significance to such an extent that it must surely have been a pre-historic retirement resort! It was also more recently plundered for alum and some extensive quarry remains are still conspicuous as they also are on Old Peak.

Ravenscar has a fickle identity and is not exactly sure of itself since its railway station closed. At the end of the last century preparations to develop it as a new resort reached an advanced stage but were never fulfilled. One suspects that the severity of its elevated position and the demands on the lungs must have been off-putting factors. However, it still boasts an hotel for the opulent and, more important, there is a strategically placed cafe providing an excellent service both to Cleveland Wayfarers and celebrating Lyke Wake Walkers whose journey across the moors from Bloworth Crossing (remember?) is now over.

The Cleveland Way turns off the old station road at Ravenscar to reach the cliff edge just south of the headland of Old Peak which effectively shuts out the view of Robin Hood's Bay. In exchange a fresh prospect stretches ahead and a first sight of Scarborough Castle distantly emphasising its headland quickens the pulse and sharpens the antcipation. Don't be fooled! With Filey Brigg, which might also be visible beyond it, it is yet another persistent image and won't be reached for some considerable time. One has first to battle through a great deal of eye-level growth first on one side of the cliff fence and then on the other by which time a point of exasperation may well have been reached! Apart from the challenge presented by overgrown and unruly vegetation there is a distinct change evident in the character of the coast south of Ravenscar. Gone for several miles are the sweeping bays and sandy beaches associated with the cliffs further north.

Instead, the coast line has a much greater regularity with boulder beaches instead of sand and the only two hints of bay formation at Hayburn and Cloughton Wykes are both poorly developed.

The change, of course, if geological. The liassic cliffs of sandstones, ironstones and their interbedded shales to the north have been exchanged for younger Middle Jurassic sandstones. Their greater uniformity and massive bedding offers a much stouter resistance to the sea and its erosion.

To a flagging walker, Scarborough Castle looks pleasantly and presently at hand but several points or small headlands soak up the miles before it is reached to say nothing of the two clefts of Hayburn and Cloughton Wyke which break the rhythm and very nearly the morale.

The actual approach to Scarborough is through Scalby Mills where the path drops down to cross the beck by a tourist styled bridge. The choice of route through the town is then open to the wayfarer as are the shops, hotels, boarding houses, cafes, pubs, cinemas, shows, amusements, bingo halls, pools, parks and public conveniences.

Scarborough is a sizeable town and while to many a Yorkshireman it is his county's answer to Blackpool on the 'other side of the hill' it is rescued by its impressive visual history, its long established fishing tradition and its fine geographical setting. Fortunately, these are virtues which no transient tourist fashion will ever subdue and so it remains an attractive place with a strong sense of identity stemming from the town and its people as much as its visitors.

340. The climb up Abbey Hill. Donkey train.

341. Some of the 199 steps up to the East Cliff.

342. Whitby. A harbour (or breath recovery) contemplation from the top of the East Cliff steps takes in the coast line back to Keldhowe Point.

343. Whitby. A slate, pantile, stack and pot contemplation from the same spot but, Oh, just look at that insensitive slick-styled modern lamp replacement set on a period standard. To introduce such an incompatible element into a close and intimate setting is a sad comment on our feeling for visual history.

344. The ruins of St. Hilda's Abbey showing the clear characteristics of Norman, Early English and Decorated Gothic styles set starkly against the sky.

345. Evidence that a good day by the sea side ....

346. is also an attraction to the aerial scavengers.

347. Public footpath to Saltwick Bay.

348. Whitby's East Cliff Skyline. A parting look back at the Abbey ruins, the farm, coastguard cottages, radio mast and look-out station.

349. Saltwick Bay caravan site.

350. The approach to the coastguard fog signal and lighthouse near Hawsker. The amplifier 'horn' of the signal is on the roof and its vocal emission which can be heard for miles around is sufficiently bovine for it to be locally named the Whitby 'bull'.

351. Coastguard station close-up. Judging by the whitewash and general level of upkeep the term Whitby Bull has another appropriate meaning!

352. The 'way' forward near Widdy Head.

354. Maw Wyke Hole. The stile and bridge over the Oakham Beck.

355. The rise from Hawsker Bottoms. On the higher ground to the right is the course of the coast railway.

356. The coast at Normanby Stye Point.

357. Bracken path across the point. The cliff rising ahead is that of Old Peak on the other side of Robin Hood's Bay over 3 miles away.

358. A picture of the coast looking back from near Craze Naze.

359. Harebell community.

360. Coastguard lookout post above Ness Point.

361. Robin Hood's Bay looking across to Old Peak and Ravenscar.

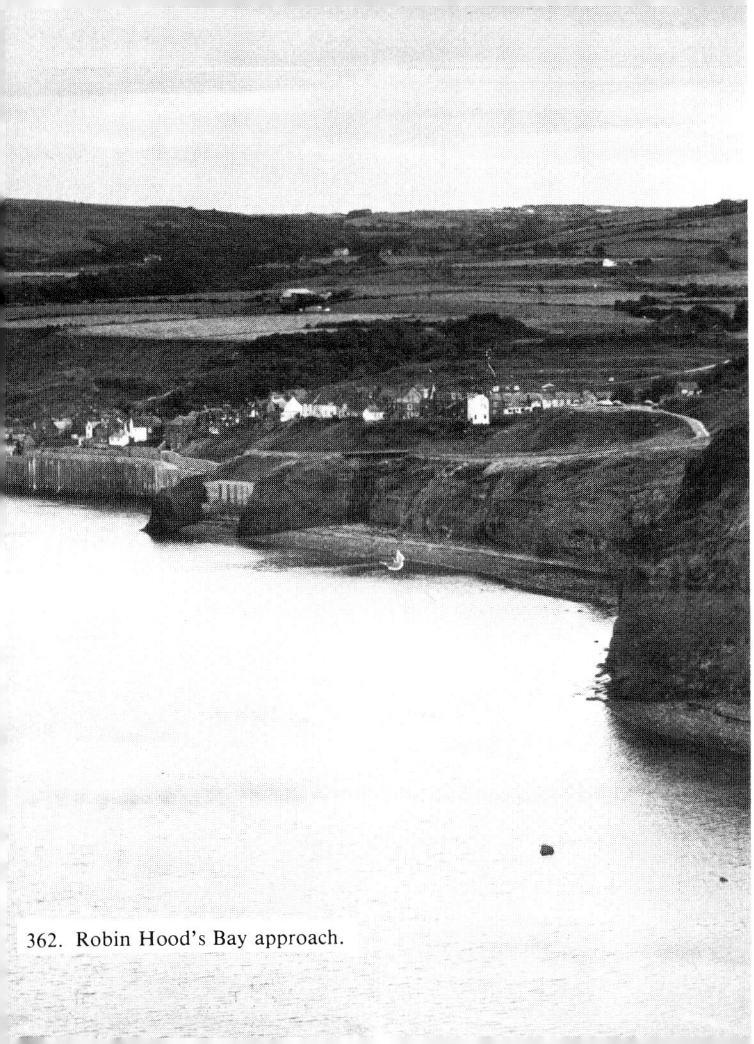

362. Robin Hood's Bay approach.

363. Robin Hood's Bay. Entry to the 'top' village from the North east.

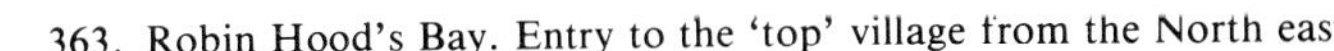

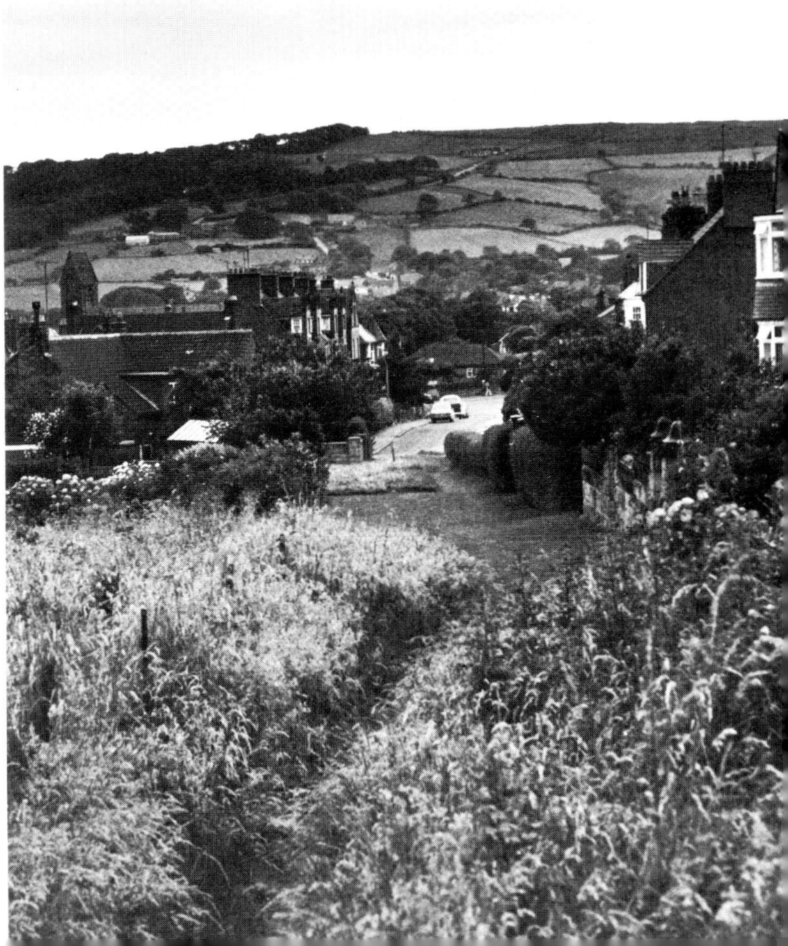

364. Robin Hood's Bay. The old fishing and sea-faring village near the water's edge.

365. Robin Hood's Bay — The Bay Hotel.

366. Robin Hood's Bay. Massive sea defences.

367. Robin Hood's Bay. Beach and boats.

368. Cautious progress over a stretch of crumbling cliff.

369. Robin Hood's Bay retrospect.

370. The bay and Old Peak from above The Sands.

371. Approach to Boggle Hole.

372. Boggle Hole beach.

373. Boggle Hole. The bridge over the Mill Beck.

374. Skirting a crop of kale the path progresses towards the Stoupe Beck. To the right above Stoupe Bank Farm rises Stoupe Brow Moor with its scars from alum quarrying clearly showing.

375. The Stoupe Beck.

376. Stoupe Bank Farm.

377. Path up Stoupe Bank.

378. Stile near Peter White cliff.

379. A selection of signs — official and unofficial.

380. Old Peak with the Raven Hall Hotel on the cliff top. On the beach immediately below are the inter tidal scars formed by resistant Lower Lias limestone bands separated by softer shales.

381. On the way up towards Brow side Farm a wide berth for a bull is accompanied by a slight rise in the adrenalin and an increase in the walking pace!

382. Cunningly concealed mushroom near Brow side Farm.

383. The shale road up to Ravenscar.

384. View east from the shale road showing the castellated walls around the grounds of the Raven Hall Hotel.

385. Looking back over Robin Hood's Bay from near the same spot.

386. Ravenscar. The strategically placed cafe.

387. Ravenscar. The return to the cliff edge.

389. A peer round the ample promontory of Blea Wyke provides another glimpse back over Robin Hood's Bay to the North Cheek.

390. A significant moment. The first sight of Scarborough Castle above the rising ground ahead also a cordial introduction to the weed 'jungle' which will be a feature of the next few miles.

391. Coastguard lookout post above Common Cliff.

392. Common Cliff and threatening skies.

393. Another sample of head-high growth together with .....

394. ...treachery underfoot. Sawn off stumps are remarkably effective in rapidly bringing the walker into a horizontal position!

395. Seascape through leaves and branches.

396. View back to Common Cliff.

397. More 'jungle' obstructions on Beast Cliff. After heavy rain the water storing propensities of this robust growth are enormous and experience suggests that it is only too pleased to transfer most of it to any luckless traveller passing through.

398. Continuing problems but this time with barbed wire assistance. Scarborough Castle on its cliff is still there but seemingly no nearer!

399. More high growth challenges on Beast Cliff. Umbels of keck.

400. North Sea peep show.

401. Drizzly advance near Rigg Hall.

402. More adversities near Red House Farm. Ahead is the cove of Hayburn Wyke followed by the gentle headlands of Tindall point, and Hundale Point.

403. Red House Farm.

404. Cliff edge Blackthorn survival near Hayburn Wyke.

405. Stile down the boulder clay banks to Hayburn Wyke.

406. Steep steps to the bridge over the Hayburn Beck.

407. Hayburn Wyke. Waterfall.

408. Hayburn Wyke public notice.

408. Hayburn Wyke public notice.

410. Hayburn Wyke. Beach and

Exit.

411. Exotic moment among the Rhododendrons.

412. Standing wheat beside the path.

413. Tindall Point. It will be noticed that Scarborough Castle is still reluctant to be approached and increasing rain has further reduced its visibility. For those who suffer from Paranoia this kind of thing can provoke a period of crisis!

414. The approach to Cloughton Wyke in even worsening visibility. The next headland is Hundale Point.

415. The huge blocks of Middle Jurassic sandstones and limestones forming the cliffs beyond Cloughton Wyke.

416. The resistant wave cut rock platform near Hundale Point.

417. Some hostile chest high vegetation near Long Nab. Bracken.

418. Creeping Thistle.

419. Strict row cabbage planting near Cloughton Field's farm.

420. Coastguard lookout post on Long Nab. A rain-filled westerly continues its onslaught.

421. From Crook Ness Scarborough cliff begins to take on a closer relationship.

422. Erosion resistance below the cliffs near Longhorn Wyke.

423. Inland water supply also near Longhorn Wyke.

424. Nearly there! Cromer Point offers a more optimistic prospect of Scalby Ness and *that* castle!

425. Cromer Point also offers a very interesting view back.

426. The tame rise over Scalby Cliff top temporarily obliterates the vision of Scarborough   but out of sight is not out of mind!

427. The gentle grade down to Scalby Mills and Scarborough's North Bay. The wayfarer has already caught up with an annual seasider who, with dog, is taking some post prandial exercise to burn up the surplus calories.

428. Entry to a tourist's world of amusements and other money relievers. On the right is the bridge over Scalby Beck.

429. Scarborough cliff and the ruin of its 12th century castle.

430. A radiant morning on Queen's Parade looking back to Scalby Ness.

431. Others looking for the Sun elsewhere!

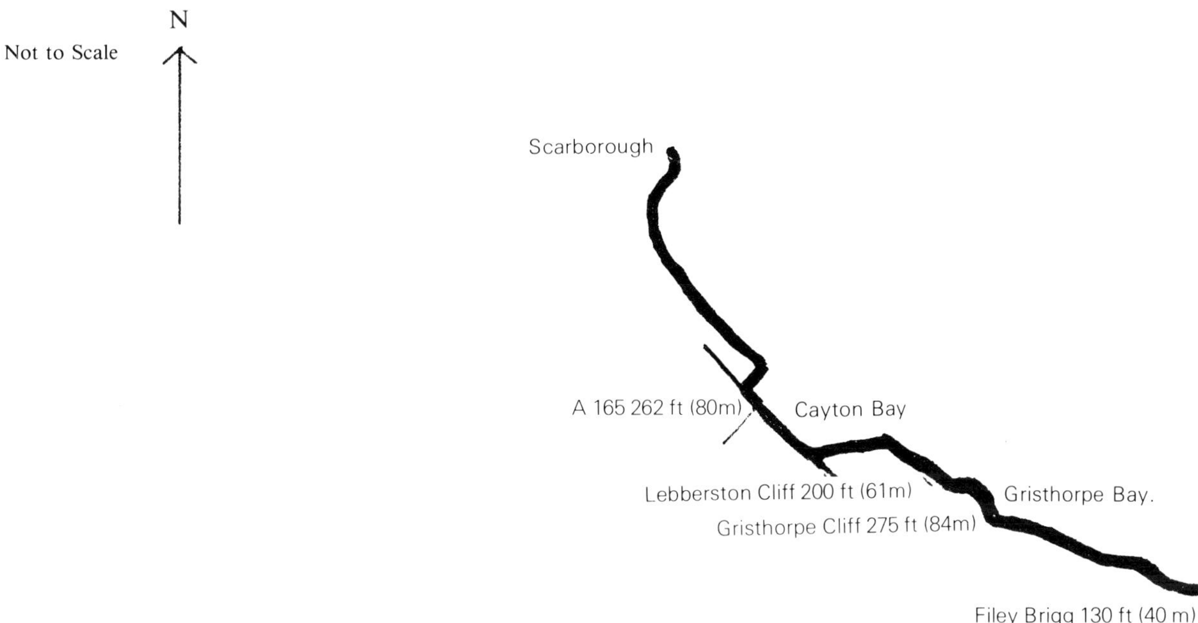

Scarborough to Filey Brigg

SCARBOROUGH TO FILEY BRIGG

9 miles (14 km)

Far from ending with the flourish that one might expect the finale of the Cleveland Way is almost an irrelevance.

It takes a long time to shake off the visible influences of Scarborough. A walk round its popular south bay is succeeded by a climb through the Spa (pronounced Spaw please!) Gardens and a stroll along the Esplanade. Residentiality gradually gives way to the golf course above Wheatcroft Cliff and then after a mini 'grovel' to cross a diminutive beck the path continues along Frank Cliff above Cornelian Bay and then turns inland to reach the main road beside the entrance to the NALGO holiday camp.

As the road runs quite close to the cliff edge here its sidewalk becomes the Cleveland Way and for nearly half a mile the walker has the opportunity to see normal people employing normal transportation techniques instead of indulging in an eccentric mode of travel involving the use of clumsy footwear. The obnoxious fumes they pump out as they pass can only be a reaction again such primitivism!

Mercifully, the path withdraws from the road again at Cayton Bay and after passing some nondescript dwellings on Killerby Cliff it improves over the last two 'official' miles. 'Official' because after covering in sequence Lebberston Cliff and Gristhorpe Cliff and then curving in sympathy with the curve of Cunstone Nab it wanders onto Newbiggin Cliff with every prospect of an exciting concluding stretch along Filey Brigg. But oh no! On Newbiggin Cliff the footpath crosses from North to East Riding and at that point the Cleveland Way formally ends and presumably the wayfarer can get out the whisky and celebrate his achievement before ignominiously finding a path into Filey or to the main road to await some wheeled deliverance.

Now whether or not a *legal* right of way exists onto the Brigg is not clear but the path certainly continues along the North Cliff and onto the Carr Naze leading to the Brigg. Thus the walker can salvage some sense of achievement and dignity by following the path to the very end where some magnificent views provide a fitting conclusion to a splendid walk.

432 Scarborough. Taking the road over the cliff. A retrospect north to Scalby Ness and Long Nab.

433. From the same spot the prospect south to White Nab and Osgoodby Point.

434. A long look at journey's end. Filey Brigg stretches out into the North Sea.

435. Scarborough. Ways down to the South Bay sea front.
A glance back up to St. Mary's parish church.

436 Narrow alley stairway to the promenade.

437 10.30am on a sun drenched morning. Money starved fruit machines and allied bandits await custom.

438. Early Bingo on the other hand has no shortage of takers.

439. Return to the 'tops' via the spa gardens on foot please...

440. No cheating like this!

441. Flora and order along the Esplanade.

442. Signposted cliff paths near South Cliff Golf Course.

443. A view back over the South Bay.

444. The coastline on to Filey Brigg from White Nab.

445. 446. Twists and undulations near Frank Cliff.

447. Main road, heavy traffic and the NALGO holiday camp.

448. The delights of the A165.

449. Cayton Bay seen from the main road.

450. A furtive shot between the cars to the low line of hills westwards. These are the chalk wolds of Flixton, Staxton and Ganton and they form the southern side of Pickering Vale.

451. The white stile that rescues the Cleveland Way from the main road and delivers it onto the top of Tennants Cliff.

452. Growth varieties at Cayton Bay. Lucerne.

453. Wild Oats.

454. Red Cliff Point with its capping of calcareous grit marks the end of Cayton Bay.

455. Looking back and down onto Cayton Bay with its mixed blessings of a splendid beach and its caravan litter.

456. Another look back at Scarborough from above Red Cliff Point.

The irregular cliff line of Filey Brigg stretching ahead from Cunstone Nab.

Some cautious well-wishing through the barbed wire.

459. Another look down the Brigg from The Wyke at the end of Gristhorpe Cliff.

460. Caravan commune near the Wyke.

461. Rubbish burn-off and another piece of
caravan landscape to the south west.

462. Filey Brigg. This photograph from near Club Point on North Cliff shows the headland narrowing along the Carr Naze. On the other side of the brigg is the sea and the distant chalk cliffs ending in Flamborough Head.

463. Beach detritus on the north side of the brigg.

464. Filey Brigg — south side.

465. Filey and Filey Bay from the Carr Naze.

466. Last lap. The sea-pounded remaining few yards.

467. A final look back along the brigg to Gristhorpe and Cayton Bays.

468. Another, by now, nostalgic look back up the north coast to Scarborough, Old Peak and even the distant tip of Robin Hood's Bay at North Cheek nearly 20 miles away.

469. The last low cliff of Filey Brigg and a farewell view of Flamborough Head.

470. The platform of calcareous grit and debris which is here at sea level fights out its last battle with the unrelenting waves.

471. Journey's end with two sizeable blisters after an unwise
change into a pair of new boots.

Maps

O.S. 1.50000 Nos   93 Tees-side & Darlington
                   94 Whitby
                   99 Northallerton and Ripon.
                   100 Malton & Pickering
                   101 Scarborough

O.S. 1 inch Tourist North York Moors

Bartholomew's ½ inch No. 36 Yorkshire Moors

Bibliography

The Cleveland Way — Alan Falconer — H.M.S.O.
The Cleveland Way — Bill Cowley — Dalesman
North York Moors National Park — H.M.S.O.
North Yorkshire Forests — Forestry Commission — H.M.S.O.
East Yorkshire & Lincolnshire — British Regional Geology — H.M.S.O.
Walking in Cleveland — Alan Falconer — Dalesman.
The Face of North East Yorkshire — Eyre & Palmer — Dalesman.
Frank Meadow Sutcliffe (An early Whitby Photographer) — Eglon Shaw — Sutcliffe Gallery, Whitby.

Youth Hostels

Helmsley, Saltburn, Whitby, Boggle Hole, Scarborough.